20/20:

We Can See Clearly Now

A journalistic view
of the year 2020
in Northern California

20/20

We Can See Clearly Now

A journalistic view
of the year 2020
in Northern California

by
Shari Rubinstein

Restoration Press
Ripples of Restoration
One Tale at a Time

Published in Roseville, California, by Restoration Press. Restoration Press is an independent publishing venture created by author Sharon Rubinstein.

Printed in the United States by Ingram/Lightning Source
Ingram/Lightning Source can be found at: www1.lightningsource.com

Library of Congress Catalog Control Number: 2023919633

Restoration Press
Ripples of Restoration
One Tale at a Time

Shari can be contacted at www.sharirubinstein.com
or shari@sharirubinstein.com

Layout and Design by Joshua Rubinstein.
Joshua can be reached at: josh@jdruby.com

Photographs of Author by Erin Ashford
Erin can be reached at e.l.ashford@gmail.com

All photos showing no photo credit were taken by Shari, Josh or Rosemary Rubinstein. All Bible references are from the King James Version except for the reference on page 16 which is taken from the New International Version.

ISBN 978-0-9986315-6-1

Rubinstein, Sharon "Shari", 1944 -
        20/20: We Can See Clearly Now / Shari Rubinstein, aka Sharon (Mings) Rubinstein
        1. Rubinstein, Shari, 1944 - 2. U. S. History, Psychology, Family, Interpersonal Relations, Social Sciences, Health, Internet

RP-0004pb

20/20

We Can See Clearly Now

The Year 2020 in Review

TABLE OF CONTENTS

IN THE BEGINNING... .... *1*

We Can See Clearly Now 3

Section A - SOCIETY & BELIEFS.................... 9

A Whole New World...11

Hemmed In, Locked Out 19

Nothing to Fear..23

Raining Ash...28

Worshipping at the Altar of Walmart..................................32

Section B - FAMILY & FRIENDS 37

Home Alone 39

All By Myself...43

It Takes Two...47

Too Close, Too Long? 50

Dinner by Design..53

Section C - SCHOOL & WORK 57

Jobs in Jeopardy 59

Technology Explosion..63

Distance Learning during COVID 68

Micah and Rory 73

The New Couch Potatoes..76

Section D - BIRTH & DEATH................................81
The Uncelebrations...83
Nuptial Nightmare..86
Baby's Born in Isolation 89
If a Graduate... 93
Silent Sendoff..98

Section E - HEARTH & HOME 103
Zoom View 105
Politics Run Amuck... 108
Under the Stethoscope... 112
Silencing the Sages 116
The Cull... 119

Section F - FUTURE & FORECAST 125
Generation "V".. 127
Doomsday Preppers Delight... 131
Turning Bad to Good 135
Breaking Free... 139
Color Me Content 143

Section G - REVIEW & RESET 147
Bright Sunshiny Day... 149
The Call 154

AND NOW ... ? 159
The Aftermath.. 161

About the Author 166

ACKNOWLEDGMENTS

My amazing family and community continue to not only be my biggest supporters, but the source of much of my inspiration.

I remain grateful for my son, Joshua Rubinstein, continuing to be my technical advisor, publicist and publisher. His design ideas are what bring this book to life. All photos are by either myself, Josh or his wife, Rosemary unless noted otherwise.

I had the excellent organizing help from two of my grandchildren, Raina Whitley and Lev Rubinstein. It is they who helped me choose and organize the photos. In addition, Lev created the first mock up for the cover from my sketches. It was his dad, Joshua, and his brother Eitan who put on the final touches. Their participation not only provided important structure, but their energy kept me on task. Thanks all!

This process has not involved my online readers as the book came so quickly I didn't even blog it as I went. Seven of my grandchildren, for whom I was supervising distance learning during this writing, were ever an encouragement and gave me the reason to put out what I believe is a timely work that affects us all, especially their generation. I am grateful they let me share bits and pieces of their stories as the pandemic and a variety of disasters have impacted their lives.

PREFACE

The idea for this book came to me in a flash. I was mulling over the many ways the diverse events of 2020 were changing our lives and, given my bent toward journalistic writing, felt the story needed to be covered.

There were several sleepless nights when specific aspects of this story were rolling around in my brain. The many scraps of paper around my bed are testimony to the organic way these perspective pieces presented themselves to me. Each piece is a work in itself, and I hope they come across as separate epiphanies on a common theme.

As we look back at human history of national and global disasters, even wars, we have endured, we realize that events of such magnitude will continue to send ripples through our society for decades, and perhaps longer. I think we can agree that we are forever changed by 2020 and it will become a benchmark by which we evaluate future calamities.

This volume offers perspective pieces that address many of the issues raised by the way our government has chosen to react to what is being called the COVID 19 pandemic. We have been at this all year and now continue into 2021.

- Shari

IN THE BEGINNING...

Clouds gathering before the storm.

Singer Johnny Nash's famous song is the inspiration for the tone of this book.

We Can See Clearly Now

We have been through a lot of grief this year. It is up to us to decide how we view this season and how we choose to go forward.

I won't be glib because I know there are those among us who have suffered the most extreme loss, whether it be from COVID, unprecedented thunder and lightning storms or the fires they started, earthquakes that chose this time to shake the earth, rioting in the streets, loss of economic stability or just the general tugging of life and death cycles exascerbated by the circumstances. What I do want to say is that we still have choice in how we hold these times in our minds.

We have experienced natural and other disasters many times throughout the years. This time we were hit with a convergence of crises that seems unequaled in our world history. Some places in the world were hit harder than others. I can only speak personally about how we were affected in northern California and America at large. Our suffering has been unprecedented for most Americans.

There's a song from 1972 by Johnny Nash – "I Can See Clearly Now" – that captures our collective mood as we hopefully are coming out of the worst of this pandemic:

I can see clearly now the rain is gone
I can see all obstacles in my way
Gone are the dark clouds that had me blind

It's gonna be a bright
Bright sunshiny day

Oh, yes I can make it now the pain is gone
All of the bad feelings have disappeared
Here is that rainbow I've been praying for

It's gonna be a bright
Bright sunshiny day

Rains can be a metaphor for any time circumstances beyond our control have threatened to inundate us. When the rains pour, it is even difficult to determine what obstacles might be in our way. The rains have now lifted. It is not that there are no problems ahead, but we can see them better now. We can plan.

Dark clouds brought the rains. It is difficult to see at all in the darkness. With the sunshine comes hope.

There has been pain in the darkness of the storm. There have been dark thoughts that now can be driven out by the coming of the light. God's sign that the storm is over – from Noah's days – is the rainbow. How we have prayed for the rainbow.

The thing I love about this old song is that it does not give the false hope that there will never be trouble again – perhaps even of the same or worse magnitude. There will not always be blue skies for us. Our paths may not be straight so that we can see very far ahead. We may not have any idea of what else can come our way. What we do know is that we who now reflect on this year made it through.

How could we have been better prepared for what just took over our world? What can we do to be ready when the next storm hits? The Doomsday preppers would tell us to keep secret stashes of food and supplies. But I would venture to say that what we just experienced made many of us realize two things.

First, we need one another. The preppers' message is just the opposite, "It's every man for himself!" As circumstances and mandates drove us away from contact with others, our hearts cried out for connection.

Many of us began our response to the mandates with being alone in our own homes, then we expanded to include our extended families in our "pod." As the months went by, some ventured out to include non-family members into their circle of contacts. Sometimes this included masking and social distancing, but we did not forsake the gathering together. (Hebrews 10:25)

Second, for those who believe in the Judeo-Christian God, there was a reaching UP combined with reaching OUT. We believe that no matter what disaster comes, God still rules. (Psalm 105:16) All of His scripture assures us that He has not stepped down from His throne. He is still in ultimate control. (Psalms 73:26)

Further, nothing can happen on earth without God's knowledge. When someone dies we say, "The Lord gives and the Lord takes away, blessed be the name of the Lord." (1 Samuel 2:6) Disasters come. But in it all, God governs them all for his wise and just and good purposes. (Isaiah 46:10)

We cannot say that the world condition we have participated in creating has not led to what we now suffer. We might want to ponder the recent worldwide crisis and determine what we can learn from it. Some are calling it a shaking. If so, toward what end? What is it that we need to be taking from our recent, and still ongoing disasters?

It seems to me that we have hopefully learned two lessons. Even though circumstances have tried to drive us away from each other and from God, we must embrace each other and our Creator.

We might have become fearful that our fellow man can infect us, or worse, attack us, which could lead us to believe the world is out of control, but we still reach out.

Further, come what may, our strength during this pandemic – and other out-of-control events with which we have been confronted – was in our urgency and effort to come together with others. There is truly strength in numbers. Whether we are shopping together, gardening, walking, worshipping, eating or just hanging out, it is being in the company of our fellow man that has brought us out of this storm, and it will again...

And ultimately, even though some believe that a loving God would not allow such suffering, there are assurances that God is indeed still in control of world events and will work all to bring eventual good from our losses. We have learned that bad things can happen to any of us, but God will not forsake us. (Deuteronomy 31:8)

I feel almost like I did when I had cataract surgery. My vision was blurred prior to the surgery and afterwards, everything was so crisp. I had not been aware of how unclearly I was seeing. I suddenly saw colors much brighter than I ever remembered seeing them. The obstacles to my physical vision had to be surgically removed.

What I see coming out of this pandemic is that we need to focus on what is important. It's inspiring how things and situations pale in comparison to being with loved ones. This pandemic has felt like surgery. The good news is that I can see what is important now. I value life more, both yours and mine. I enjoy spending time with my family and friends.

Together, we will not just survive, but thrive.

-A-

SOCIETY & BELIEFS

Like a stormy sky the pandemic threatened our very lives.

My local bank had to accept "masked" customers,
socially distanced, of course.

A Whole New World?

This year has presented worldwide pandemonium in every aspect of life – the COVID 19 pandemic being the major disaster, still ongoing at this writing. Restrictions are happening globally to stem the impact of this mystery virus. In America, our local, state and national governments have exerted control over all our movements ostensibly to slow down the number of people contracting the deadly virus.

In my former life as a high school English teacher,

I taught Aldous Huxley's Brave New World, written in 1932, almost 70 years ago. It was presented as a cautionary tale depicting a dystopian, totalitarian society in which "individual liberty has been usurped by an all-powerful state." Not my words.

The message of Huxley's futuristic society is to warn mankind of the dangers of giving the state absolute control over human beings, especially by their controlling "new and powerful technologies." This myopic government views the problems of society as having been generated by human relations gone awry, causing people to be very unhappy. The state's goal is to regulate human happiness. The problem, of course, is that happiness is an individual thing. One size does not fit all.

It is very revealing for readers to note what words are considered obscene in this distorted society. In the Brave New World the worst word is "mother." Similarly, "dirty" words in this New World are "father," "born," "parents" and any intimate family relationship title. Personal connections are strictly forbidden.

It's easy to see that none of these words are ever used because no one is allowed to have a baby. The state sterilizes two-thirds of the women right after birth because their technology has developed to the extent that they can produce a lot of humans with only one egg. The resultant beings are actually clones, mentally and physically. This "futuristic" intervention developed people to be content in whatever "class" for which they have been engineered.

They surgically remove women's ovaries if they need to "bottle" new children. All offspring are test tube babies. No child ever has any idea of who his or her parents are. There is no such concept.

If persons begin to think for themselves – ultimately, naturally, forming relationships with others – they are considered savages and are sent to a reservation, hopefully prior to their having any subversive influence on others.

And now here we are in the 21st Century. We can agree that most of the struggles mankind has is in its relationships with each other. We read statistics indicating that the institutions we put in place to alleviate dysfunctional relationships don't necessarily have a high success rate.

We have men and women in a battle of the genders. Gender dysmorphia is at an all-time high, but now is legally construed as normal. We contend with parents who can't nurture their children. We have people not respecting others' property at an all-time high. Our social and judicial systems are overrun with petitions, court cases, welfare decisions, all to try to cause people to make nice.

What to do? It is tempting to want to control everyone. In fact, the Creator could have pre-programmed us to do "right" at all times. Instead, He formed us with the freedom to choose our path for ourselves. We don't always make the best decisions, but that does not give anyone license to force others to do what they might believe is best. We are free to try to influence others, even educate others, but no individual nor entity has the right to usurp God-given free will.

American society struggles in how to govern itelf. We are given a democratic process whereby we get to vote officials into their positions, but once they are in power, our check and balance system cannot curtail abuse of power without petitioning to remove the person from his or her post – a daunting, complex, multi-faceted task. Politicians of every ilk vie for their disparate positions to be the law of the land.

So, the year is now 2020. Enter stage left, the coronavirus. Our technology is not advanced enough yet to combat many viruses. This one appears especially virile. I qualify this because the public gets conflicting "authoritative" statistics on the course, hence danger, of this virus. Pronouncements are made and then countered by an updated view within days or weeks. Each time, the public is cautioned how they are to respond to the situation for the good of all.

Then the cautions turned to mandates. We were under house arrest for months. When we were allowed out, we were instructed to keep a six-foot distance from others and for all to wear masks. Massive restrictions of every activity were put in place often with the threat of huge fines or arrests for offenders.

Case in point occurred when a small part of my family got the opportunity to take a road trip to a beach town. Signs were plastered everywhere on the beach proclaiming that there was a $100 fine for anyone not wearing a mask. A law enforcement person was stationed close by to issue tickets as warranted.

Only what the government determined to be "essential" places of business could be open. No more haircuts. No movie theaters. No school. Not even any parks. No restaurants. No places of worship. Most places of retail business shut down or were under severe "social distancing" restrictions, which took a lot of scrambling to provide so they could have customers, hence a living.

All during 2020 regulations kept changing and continue to do so into 2021. Establishments were open, closed again, opened partially, closed again. At first restaurants could only serve outdoors and with social distancing. Then they could have limited inside distance dining. Then it was withdrawn to only order out. At this writing diners can only get take out, no eating inside or outside.

Many hair salons have gone underground, brown

papering their windows, locking their doors, and asking patrons to text when present so they can quickly admit them. It was six months before I got a haircut and then I was concerned my hairdresser might get arrested. Tapping on her salon door felt much like what I imagine it was like to seek entrance to speakeasies – secret establishments serving liquor from 1919 to 1933 during America's Prohibition against the sale of alcohol. My salon's prohibited product? A haircut.

Schools in our state were not allowed to reopen, setting up distance learning instead. Predominantly two-working-parents' households scrambled to provide adult supervision for their children sequestered at home doing schoolwork on "chromebooks." It's anybody's guess how many children have been home alone. We used to only be concerned about those kids left unsupervised between school dismissal and parents coming home from work. During this pandemic there could be any number of children left home all or most of the day without adult attention.

There has been a huge negative impact on the economy with many workers losing their livelihood from their places of business being limited or shut down. Some have been sent home to accomplish their work assignments on their computers. There's a mixed review of this arrangement.

Many places of business deemed "non-essential" have permanently shut their doors. When I look at any strip mall in my area, most of these store-fronts are plastered with closed signs. They ranged from shoe repair to jewelry and even nail salons.

Likewise, faith-based institutions are not allowed to open which has greatly reduced their ability to receive their usual funding – hence threatening their viability – not to mention their congregants being denied access to in-person spiritual counsel for their COVID-troubled lives.

A colleague noted, however, "God was able to greatly increase the impact of ministries around the world, including Israel, during this COVID 19 lockdown." (Dana Sudborough) Organizations like Tree of Life Ministries-Israel reported that in 2020 they had an "explosion of video views...reaching 23 million."

This sounds exactly like what is referenced in Isaiah 59:19: "When the enemy comes in like a flood, the Spirit of the Lord will lift up a standard against him." In this context, standard refers to a flag or banner. In military terms, the flag precedes the army, announcing the arrival of those who will do battle. The good news is that God will find a way to bring a holy outcome into the darkest earthly circumstance.

Beyond the financial decline and the spiritual threat, the impact on limited socializing will be far-reaching. People are very isolated. Yes, they are having meetings online. Yes, they are making phone calls. But there is no substitute for personal contact.

There is possibly one other good thing to come out of this. With many parents having to stay home to either do their work or wait for when they can get work again, families have reportedly been spending more time together. Given the financial stress and cabin fever, however, it can be questioned how positive having extended time in close quarters has been.

So what am I advocating? First, we must question why there were mandates circumventing personal choices. Are there people who will make bad decisions? Yes, but frankly – and historically – they are not likely deterred by mandates.

Second, even recommendations of changes in behavior should take into consideration those who are truly the most vulnerable. Should no one get to go shopping, go to school, go to work, go to religious services if there are a few, such as I, who cannot due to age or impaired health?

Third, deciding what services are essential should not be a political football. The places shut down are often offering the things that provide us with quality of life that makes life worth living.

Shades of <u>Brave New World</u> that abortion clinics have remained open!

Fourth, and probably most important, politicians must keep their personal aspirations out of sifting through the "scientific" information. To make informed choices, we the people need actual, verifiable data, not what any political figure might think will further his or her own rise to power.

It had been predicted we might not have any solid solution – which was touted as a vaccine for COVID – until the summer of 2021. At this edit – December 20, 2020 – the first vaccines have been released to the healthcare professionals' tier of essential workers. To the credit of this administration's effort – still under President Trump – laboratories and governing medical agencies have pushed the vaccine's creation and distribution just in time for our yearly flu season spike.

Let it be said, however, there is a large contingency who are very skeptical about the safety of the new vaccine. For these people, they are busy researching how to beef up their immune systems to either avoid getting the virus, or at least minimizing its power over them.

Do we even know how many actual coronavirus cases there are? With the regular flu having similar symptoms to COVID 19, there is the danger of the incidences of the yearly flu being mistakenly reported as cases of the coronavirus which can swell those numbers by which authorities are making decisions for public mandates.

All in all, we already have sufficient hindsight to realize data gathering and interpretation as well as communications about the extent and danger of the coronavirus, have been grossly mishandled during this year. Frankly, We, the People, have been mishandled. At this point we have all been forced to forge a "new normal." But, it is neither new nor normal. It is the same old game.

Politicians make every effort to control the information to serve their party's prowess. Neither side of the aisle was able to gain our confidence that it had our best interests at heart. This pandemic happening in an election year has been devastating.

Political football is not a game anyone can win, but in this case, the People are the ones taking all the hits.

Grandson Micah puts masks to good use.
Remember when the superheroes all wore masks?
MICAH MAN comes to save the day! If only he could...

Hemmed In, Locked Out

These are extraordinary times. Most of us have never found our world to be so constricted.

Sometimes we talk about the familiar Disney motto, "It's a Small World," but usually that is in reference to how much our own little worlds are like everyone else's. It's an expression that captures our connectedness no matter where we live, who we are. We are more alike than we are different. That is a positive.

During the times of this pandemic, all of our "worlds" have become very small in the negative sense. We live in tiny bubbles and are mandated to stay there, not making connections with others. The fear driving the mandates is that this hateful virus will spread and remain virulent the more we have personal interaction with our fellow human beings.

When COVID 19 went full-blown, world, national, state, county and city directives came down forcing people to withdraw in every area of their lives. I have already mentioned many of them, but I find it especially sad that even all public parks were closed. Only work that could be accomplished via computer was allowed. There was no human contact except for what were deemed essential services.

In the beginning of this pandemic, the businesses allowed to remain open included those providing food, fuel for our vehicles and only urgent health care. The establishments that delivered these needs had to figure out how to provide what was required and still not allow contact that could make people vulnerable to receiving or transmitting the virus. Hence the term coined, "social distancing."

There were extra precautions for the elderly and heath-compromised individuals. Many of the over-65 group expressed not feeling safe leaving their homes at all so their needed commodities had to come to them. Grocery stores began to deliver food to any who could not go out. For those visiting their stores, they provided clear, consumer-friendly signage to direct customers on how to keep the required six-foot distance. Some products were no longer being offered as they would have involved shoppers sharing uncovered food served directly by employees such as hot samples and even deli meals.

Due to the need for heightened cleanliness, cleaning

products were in great demand. Stores could not keep up and ran out of many necessary items. It's now a joke that there was a run on toilet paper, but at the time this product was scarce reportedly primarily due to hoarding. Interesting to note that just days before the end of 2020, due to the latest spike in corona, there is another shortage of paper products.

Social distancing and the wearing of masks were strictly enforced at health care facilities and only persons having urgent needs were permitted. No one could accompany another into the ER, for example, unless that person could not speak for him or herself. Even dental offices cancelled all routine cleanings. Terminally-ill patients often faced dying alone.

Patients were encouraged to get their usual meds online and to put off all non-emergency appointments and procedures. Anyone entering medical facilities was quizzed about any recent fever or coughing. Even now – at this edit in the fall of 2022 – some clinics continue to take the temperature of anyone seeking entry.

It's interesting to think about how people who normally never went out much at all also feel overwhelmed by the forced isolation. It's not just the fact that we can't go out, but that it is mandated that we can't. No casual running to the store for a couple of items. No inviting someone over on the spur of the moment. No running next door for a cup of sugar. It's not that we did those things much, but it's the reality that now we couldn't if we wanted to. That's what gets to us.

In the final analysis, it's about feeling controlled. We want to be in charge of our own lives. Even as young kids, we often assert ourselves against parental rules. We might have wanted to do exactly what they asked, but we don't want to be told what to do or not do. Mom: "Why don't you grab an ice cream bar, Dear?" Kid: "No thanks, I'm not hungry." Ha.

How much did the authorities making all the rules during this pandemic consider this very essential part of our innate nature? Who tells a whole nation to not leave their houses, not see their families or friends? What great mind thought up this plan of action for getting conformity?

No clear-thinking person, especially not one who understands human nature, would ever set up overarching rules that beg to be defied. After all, even God realized that His Ten Commandments posed a barrier to compliance. Posting rules has the human effect of causing curiosity as to why the rule. Remember Adam and Eve?

This whole pandemic could/should have been handled differently. I know there will always be people who won't comply no matter what. But does anyone really believe they will somehow magically do the right thing when locked down? A coerced people can become a crazed people. There are those so focused on how to get around the rules that they don't think clearly.

Having been a teacher for 40 years, I realized early on that you don't organize your class based on your "bad actors." You don't make rules to try to coerce behavior. Explain what is needed to those who truly want to understand the why's and suggest to them some well-documented, research-endorsed best practices. Consequence or restrict only those who don't comply and let the others continue.

If we had suggestions or guidelines rather than mandates, perhaps we could have had much more compliance and buy-in. It's all in how it gets presented. Don't treat everyone as if they are naughty children looking to defy the rules. Give us credit for caring as much or more than the authorities about how this pandemic plays out.

In the words of an old western movie, "Don't fence us in."

Random violence, my truck's window shattered by a BB gun assailant in the night.

"We have nothing to fear but fear itself."

U.S. President Franklin D. Roosevelt was quoted as making this statement in his inaugural address in March of 1933, in which he was declaring war on the Great Depression. He knew all too well the danger of fear.

My parents were young adults during the Great Depression. I have heard the stories. The similarity to what we are experiencing in this corona pandemic is unsettling. Just as FDR knew how much more devastating their plight would be if they succumbed to fear, it is equally important for us to remember during these trying times.

The experts in every area of our lives are lined up to let the American people – and even the world population – know how devastating this pandemic will be to our lives. Many have projected that we are heading to another Great Depression which economically affects all strata of life. Much of the media is playing a significant role in keeping fear whipped up. "If it bleeds it leads" has always been the media's motto. Leave it to them to capture the worst statistics, often ignoring or minimizing any positives.

Some forecasters have thrown out a ray of hope for there to be an immediate economic upsurge as the virus begins to wane, but they predict the long-term effects will keep rippling. Just as the Great Depression was full blown in the 1930's, this one is thought to go into full effect into the 2030's, making it 100 years between major US economic downturns.

Everything we are hearing is supposition. Not one so-called authority can say for sure exactly what will happen. Not knowing how bad things could get can cause serious concern. The nature of fear is to grab hold of our hearts and minds. We are definitely in a battle.

There are many variables, not the least of which is what we the people will do in the face of these predictions. None of the naysayers are accounting for the indomitable power of the human spirit. We are not victims. We were created in the image of our God.

Fear can happen when there is the unknown or the terrible known, or a combination of both. There is nothing our Creator does not know. We mere mortals try to keep moving forward, sometimes apprehensive of what might be around the next corner. He has told us not to fear but to trust in Him. He is the provider of peace and sanity. (Phillipians 4:7-8)

For us, this pandemic brings both the familiar and unfamiliar. What we know is there is the coronavirus. It is unlike any we have seen. We hear of its devastating impact worldwide. But there are many unknowns associated with it. It has taken about nine months for medical research to create a vaccine for this virus. Here at the end of 2020, the vaccine is being given to only the highest tier of "essential" workers. The wait for all to be inoculated is projected to be in middle to late 2021. And there are still those who will never take the vaccine.

As we know, persons 65 and older or those with any kind of compromised health issues are more at risk for both catching the virus and succumbing to it. The media keeps up a daily – many times conflicting – barrage of local, national and world statistics on how many of this demographic has been affected.

We have been told masks are imperative. As I used to tell my students – and my own children – the speaking voice goes up to six feet and a cough or sneeze goes 16 feet. Hence the social distancing of at least six feet. A mask hopefully contains the occasional bursts of breath.

Here in northern California we had been struck simultaneously with dry thunder and lightning storms that caused unprecedented wildfires. The bad air ratings went all the way to "hazardous" levels all across the state and miles beyond. We heard news reports that our smoke reached the east coast and even Europe.

When residents could no longer eat outside due to dangerous air quality, the restaurants were "miraculously" reopened for inside eating. The fact that authorities could suddenly decide it was safe to eat indoors again seemed very arbitrary.

Perhaps the back and forth of social "norms" is the

most unsettling. It's no wonder that we have so many control freaks. If we can make things happen by our own volition, even to the extent of manipulating circumstances and people, we hope we will be safe, successful, loved.

But in the face of it all, we need to first keep it in perspective. How many disasters have we faced and overcome? I've lived long enough to have quite a history of facing down adversity. I have experienced the truth that things will get better. I am sure we all have.

I know that we often suffer needlessly worrying what might or might not come. As Jesus says at the end of the Sermon on the Mount (Matthew 6:34): "Therefore do not worry about tomorrow, for tomorrow will worry about itself. Each day has enough trouble of its own."

Anticipating trouble can be worse than the thing itself. I heard a Christian radio station announcer yesterday talk about how he and his wife were to be tested for corona. They were not looking forward to it, having heard some harrowing reports of Q-tips being shoved up noses seemingly to the brain. Once they were finally at the test center, the nurse completed the procedure so quickly, they didn't have time to react. They both reported it was nowhere near as bad as what they had dreaded.

Forewarned is forearmed. We count on hearing the facts of a situation so we can weigh how we should prepare. Sadly, as I have reported, we keep getting mixed messages that keep us from being able to do even fundamental planning. We should have an idea of how we are moving forward, but there are always many variables, obstacles that can thwart even our best-laid plans. Being overly concerned about what might come can actually raise blood pressure. Common fact: stress can be a killer.

The onset of stress is not restricted to real danger. When I was a kid, I loved watching scary movies. Sometimes I had to actually run out of the room or into the lobby of the theater when the "threat" became intense. My pulse raced. My heart pounded. My brain sent a message: "Danger, run away." Intellectually, I knew it was only a movie, but because my senses didn't know the difference and instead registered real danger, my mind acted accordingly. So, we are even fearful of what we can imagine might happen. Our bodies still register our concerns as if they were actually already happening.

We may not even realize that our minds are holding on to the fear of danger. That is why we know to "Let this mind be in you that is also in Jesus the Messiah." (Philippians 2:5) Does Jesus fear the virus, or whatever disaster presents itself? How could He? He is the Lord of all and has assured us that if we believe in Him, whatever He did while on earth, we can do that and more. (John 14:12-14) He speaks to demons and they depart, He drives diseases out of bodies, He speaks to the winds and they become calm. We can speak to this pandemic.

So, in the final analysis, how do we keep our heads when everyone around us is losing theirs? We realize that we are not alone, adrift on this earth. We ask for heavenly guidance to interpret the signs. We are assured our Father will never leave us nor forsake us. When He said this, He could see into the future and knew every trial that would come.

And above all, He knows how the story ends – He wins! When He wins, so do we.

The ash falling from the fires in northern California forced us all indoors.

It's Raining Ash

These are very troubling times. The pandemic has been enough of a disaster, but here in northern California, we also have the wildfires with which to contend. Dry thunder-lightning storms brought thousands of lightning strikes, resulting in a record-setting number of wildfires. Half the acreage of a nearby city was engulfed in flames. Massive fireballs shot up everywhere, defying the weary firefighters.

Fires wreak such havoc. There is, of course, the physical damage of the flames, but the smoke from burning forests blankets entire sections of the state. National weather services track the bad air, assigning numbers related to how dangerous they are. Anywhere in the low 100's is unhealthy for sensitive groups and under 200 affects even those not in a sensitive group. A couple of days ago we registered over 400 on this scale. It was considered hazardous to all life.

God is very aware of how all of these disasters affect us. Sometimes I wish we could regularly see the angels that are promised us in the scriptures. I think we would be amazed how many times the Lord has preserved our lives.

My son-in-law, Aaron, is the City Manager of the burning town I mentioned. From the command post, he and other city officials were closely monitoring the fires and directing the response efforts. Feeling they needed to see for themselves to better direct the emergency services, Aaron and the Fire Chief drove to inspect a hot spot of the fire. As they were noting the magnitude of the damage, a 40-foot wall of fire instantly arose and literally chased them back to their vehicles. They miraculously escaped unscathed.

About a week later, the officials of the town in which I live – about an hour east of the city just described – decided to do a controlled burn of the fields around the city because the fields are overgrown with dry brush this time of year. Even though they were hoping to avert fires that could threaten people and property, these fires doubled the amount of smoke in the air. I give our town officials credit for then hiring goatherds to bring in their flocks that are numbered in the hundreds to graze off some of these fields that are wedged in with homes and businesses.

Regardless, the end result was a new wave of hazardous air. I purchased medical grade masks for wearing outdoors. I make every effort to keep my doors and windows shut, but there is a fair amount of smoke that still gets in. I bought a room air purifier that is supposed to keep the air clean. I keep it in whatever room I am using at the time.

My high school-teacher son Josh has been broadcasting his distance learning to his students from the school. On the day of the heaviest smoke, he dismissed his students from their online class so he could go home as the smoke had penetrated his classroom.

The sun was an eerie hazy orange that day. Dusk was actually a couple of hours early. When the moon came up it was ringed with a heavy shroud of ash particles.

My ten-year old grandson Lev has breathing issues. Everything about the pandemic and the fires has been a major threat to his health. I am with him and his three siblings a couple of days a week to help them with their mandated distance learning. I have noticed that his breathing is beginning to be impaired.

This grandson also has a 20-month-old sister Ava who can't really be masked – which is also true of the brother – so there is not much protection for her either. The parents found a nearby daycare for this little one as it was impossible to give her full attention when helping the other four children do their schoolwork from home while maintaining their own jobs. Most of little Ava's classmates are wearing masks. They do not get to play outside.

I was speaking to a friend on the telephone last night who has been under her doctor's care for smoke inhalation damage. She is a healthy middle-aged woman with no history of cigarette smoking nor asthma. When the skies first became hazy with smoke she said she thought it was like being around a campfire so wasn't alarmed. Then she realized she could not escape the smoke. It even leaked into her home though all the windows were tightly closed.

We don't have any reports yet on how much lasting damage has been caused by the wildfire smoke. When some of my relatives in other states have heard of our California wildfires in other years, they called with concerns for our safety and that of our property. Through the years they have asked about the smoke in the air which historically has not rivaled the fire itself. This year, however, the smoke damage has equaled that of the actual fires.

Even in a non-pandemic year, our fires would be considered a health emergency. The wildfires have dominated up and down our coastline. Coupled with corona, those of us living in this part of the U. S. seem to be being attacked inside and out.

Even for those who believed all the restrictions were necessary precautions during COVID 19, the imperatives to stay indoors impacted us all. We west coasters are further compelled to stay inside by the unavoidable danger of the very air we breathe.

We realize that the sun is helping eradicate the virus. We are torn because it is rain we need to put out the fires and clear the air. I am reminded of the poet Robert Frost posing a dilemma of whether people would die from fire or from ice. For us it is fire or virus. Not much of a choice, as both are lethal.

For now, we must cry, "Bring on the rains!"

While our congregation's Rabbi live streamed our services from his living room, our local Walmart was jammed packed.

Worshipping at the Altar of Walmart

Does it seem incongruous? To me, too. But, we are in a time when faith communities are forbidden to meet indoors at all but the Walmarts of the world are open for business. In fact, the parking lots of such places are as full as before COVID 19. Supposedly shoppers are social-distanced and masked, but at any given time an observer will note that neither is routinely happening.

It is not only a sign of the COVID Times, but a move toward devaluing faith in a Creator, an omnipotent God.

Major shopping outlets are open but faith communities are told to shut down or risk penalties or even incarceration. Faith leaders in this country wrestled with this mandate. Entire organizations shut down, but others chose civil disobedience and kept their doors open. These were tense times.

Religion has been relegated to a low place on the essential business list. What has become of our society that used to be characterized as a Judeo-Christian nation? Our center has shifted.

There is no consensus among our government officials about what constitutes essential services. I heard a typical hypocritical anecdote about the mayor of Chicago, who had supported the closing of hair and nail salons, but was secretly getting her hair done. Her response when confronted by the public was, "In my job, I have to keep up a good appearance." I'd say her keeping up appearances is more about who she is than what she looks like.

Does she not understand that everyone feels better when they can look their best? She should have been trying to help figure out how everyone could access this service as an essential part of our lives. Moreover, how about all those barbers and hairdressers who no longer have a livelihood?

The situation we have where Big Government is dictating what the masses can and cannot do is so reminiscent of a book most of us studied in school, Animal Farm. Do you remember how the animals took the farm away from the farmer and started off chanting that every animal is "equal" to everyone else, but that there had to be some people in charge. By the end of the story those in charge had given themselves permission to take on all the behaviors they previously opposed in their oppressive former owners. The "boss" animals were evidently more equal than others.

Think of things you would consider essential to your well being. Are you finding that the various closures influenced by health "authorities" and dictated by those in charge match your own? What has been prohibited that has impacted your quality of life?

At this most troubling time in our recent history, when we need to be able to not only connect with each other but with our God, we are hindered from both. The congregation I attend has already been broadcasting its services and has continued through this pandemic. I think I can speak for both the leadership – of which I am one – and the congregants when I report that being able to only access my faith community remotely, feels just that – remote.

Our leader actually felt the need to challenge the online followers to be as intentional as possible when we gather online. He was addressing the fact that many were not even getting dressed to meet with everyone in the cloud. His efforts were well-intentioned, but it challenges our imaginations to think ourselves into a sanctuary with like-minded believers when in reality we are sitting on our couches or even in our beds while "listening" to the service.

It is a challenge for worshippers to avoid developing a consumer, audience mentality even when they are sitting in the actual sanctuary. Leadership in all our faith communities want congregants to fully participate, rather than just receive and perhaps check off "did service today." During this pandemic, congregants have acquired a new level of passivity and this at the very time when we are most in need of divine intervention and consolation.

Where does our help come from? Certainly not from our elected and appointed officials. We need help from a much higher level. We need to be able to have our faith built during this time, for it is faith that is the opposite of fear. As we know, fear of what might come can be as damaging as encountering the actual event. We need faith that the One who created us will see us through, regardless of how crazy things might get.

We need to be in the same room with fellow believers to lift our voices corporately in praise and worship for we "enter His gates with thanksgiving and into His courts with praise." (Psalm 100:4) It is in His presence that we will have peace. It happens within each believer, but we reach Him when we lift our voices in one accord.

Businesses such as Walmart that are open to us are the very places where it is every person for him or herself, not a place to congregate and engage with one another. They are places that encourage our separation from our fellow man when the opposite is needed.

If God had intended for everything to fall into place in isolation, He wouldn't have made anyone beyond Adam. He wouldn't have provided a way to populate the earth and give the command for people to multiply.

Man was never intended to be an island.

-B-

FAMILY & FRIENDS

Storm brewing in my neighborhood.

FIDDYMENT RD

RED LIGHT
VIOLATION
$ 479

On a rare day when some of us got to go to our local park,
Grandson Lev was left with no one with whom to play.

All Alone

I grew up amongst six siblings. I was rarely alone. I spent a lot of my youth trying to get some time to myself, to no avail. The togetherness wasn't all bad. My sibs and I entertained each other.

I slept in a bed with one or two of my sisters all my childhood. Sometimes all five sisters climbed into one bed for back rubs. We had it all worked out. We would all turn the same direction so that each of us could rub a back while receiving one from the sister behind us.

The one at the end of the line, however, knew she would only get her back massaged every other time, but she had opted for this so when she was receiving she could relax and enjoy it. We called it "tickle, pat, rub" as we each got to choose the kind of back rub we wanted.

By this time our oldest brother was living with his maternal grandparents, but the youngest in the family is the second son. He was always a bit young for our shenanigans but we included him when we could. He had to suffer being the baby when we played "house." We played with neighbors also, but our main playmates were our own siblings.

The point of all this is that none of us was ever alone. It made it more shocking when I married and moved away from my family. I'm not sure I would have described my condition as lonely, but I did feel alone.

I worked full time while simultaneously earning college degrees and parenting my three children and later a step-child. I never made even one lasting friend at my work places nor schools. I had a short stint as a hippie and made a few lifetime friends then, but we were only together a few short years. Now we live several states – and even a continent – away from each other.

My best friends now are in my faith community. Somehow it seems that even those with whom I am closest are not always in sync with me, nor I with them. It is definitely not the unconditional love I experienced with my siblings.

I don't think I am alone – no pun intended – in feeling this way. Close connections are important to life. I think that is why the whole pandemic sequestering – house arrest – hit so hard. The worst thing you can do to human beings is to deprive them of having up-close-and-personal contact with their loved ones. We thrive with touch, wither without.

I watch many on Facebook connecting virtually with their friends and families. I observed a friend in Israel with her two children talking through a plate glass with the grandparents. I hear the cries of many lonely people, reaching out, trying to cope.

We lock up people who have committed crimes. Being away from their friends and families takes the biggest toll on human emotions. When prisoners get busted for bad behavior, they receive the maximum cruelty – being put in Solitary.

I think we can see that it doesn't take guns or massive explosions to bring a nation to its knees. You can scare them enough that they will willingly stay away from others. You can continue the isolation perhaps long past the need.

Granted, we have learned from historical plagues and other biological disasters that we must separate the infected from those who are not, at least while procuring vaccines and other treatments. This particular pandemic, however, bred a worldwide hysteria even among officials. The question arises, "Could they have let us outside sooner than they did?"

As speaker Garrison Keillor was quoted as saying, "Social isolation breeds contempt." We can lose empathy for others with whom we have no close contact. As Keillor elaborated, "The bombardier never sees the quiet shady street of brick houses that he is about to incinerate." Likewise during these times we have seen an escalation in man's inhumanity to man.

Twenty-two centuries ago Julius Caesar said, "Divide and conquer." If we can create dissension in the ranks, to use a military term, we can dismantle the entire army and win the war as Caesar did to conquer Gaul. As pointed out by God (Matthew 12:25): "Every kingdom divided against itself is brought to desolation, and every city or house divided against itself will not stand."

Even though people say we enter and leave this life alone, that is not exactly accurate. We are usually in the company of close friends and family. This pandemic has touched a universal human nerve. It has robbed us of closeness in birth and death and all activities in between.

Divided we fall, BUT united we stand is the expression attributed to the Greek storyteller Aesop. True that.

Three grandsons still in their jammies, building Legos: Micah, Lev, Eitan.
A favorite way to pass the time in confinement.

All By Myself

There have been various types of isolation during this pandemic. Those who live alone or those who are part of a very small family have a more difficult time.

In the beginning, when we were first ordered to stay in our own homes, I would hear tales of people trying to make the best of it. Most of us have so many "honey do" projects requiring attention that we took the isolation as a mixed blessing. As a nation – nay, a world – we have to be SO spruced up by now.

Buildings were painted inside and out, gardens plant-
ed and tended, sewing projects at last crossed the finish
line to completion. I even know of chicken coops being
built. Long forgotten items in attics and basements have
been uprooted and summarily discarded or rehomed.
Closets, pantries and cabinets have order restored at
last. Projects that had been awaiting a rainy day, or even
a day off, were clumped together and vied for our attention. All worthy endeavors. Idle hands committed to the
tasks.

After a few months, however, with no end to the pandemic in sight, nerves began to fray. We are reminded of
the well-known proverb from James Howell's collection
in 1659, "All work and no play makes Jack a dull boy."
Dull indeed.

Not everyone had the "luxury" of cleaning out closets
and such. Many were home, but not in leisure. Places of
employment were forced to have as many as possible
working from their homes. Some loved this arrangement, until they realized that the only connection they
would have with their colleagues was virtual. This made
for lonelier jobs, but also less efficient. Not everything
can be relegated to online interaction.

Many parents who formerly went out for work were
now home, but those with school-age children were put
in the position of trying to juggle work and supervise
their children doing school at home. My son-in-law Michael already had a job working at home. His wife, my
daughter, Sarah travels out to assignments that keep her
absent from home most hours of the day.

They have four children, three of whom are in elementary and middle school. Someone has to supervise
their learning at home. The oldest child is in college –
virtually – and also has a job so is not available to help
with his siblings.

I assist two days a week – splitting my time between their house and that of my son Josh's family. The other three days, Michael gets up very early so he can work for several hours allowing him time to keep tabs on his little learners throughout the day. Not ideal, but we all make it work.

As alluded to previously, many children are without any adult supervision. We just have to remember the somewhat fanciful popular movie "Home Alone" to realize the depths of troubles unattended children can get into. I am certain less learning is going on and the danger of bored little minds cast loose in their houses conjures up all sorts of potential hazards.

So, homes are full, businesses are empty, some essential supplies have been rationed, businesses – and schools – are being yo-yoed back and forth on opening partially or not at all for the foreseeable future.

There are some who would cite the side benefits of so many rarely leaving their homes: vehicle fuel savings, fewer driving accidents, money saved not eating out, better air quality as vehicles sit idle, less need for "public" clothing or appearance – did I mention how many work at their computers in their jammies?

On the surface, one might be tempted to see these benefits as offsetting the damages of sequestering, but the negative repercussions are too many. How have the businesses providing all the goods and services been affected? There has been massive loss of revenue, debilitating diminishing of wages and even jobs lost.

I suspect that any worker who ever complained about going to work sees things differently now. I am even hearing kids begging to go to school! Who would have thought there could be such a turnaround? Shift a paradigm and watch the scramble.

A continuing concern has been that home becoming the center of all work and school could be our new norm? At the very least, school districts and businesses – having put in so much energy to move us all home – may not be eager to return to their former condition.

There are some definite advantages to work remaining at home, at least part-time. Employers and employees alike have seen that much of what they do does not require large physical facilities nor continual personal interaction. I suspect many will continue working at home.

I am less enamored with children learning at home, unless there is a committed adult ready to guide their education. Families who were already home schooling were doing so by choice. Those who chose for their children to be educated away from home many times made this decision since all adults were pursuing their giftings and callings working outside the home, or taking care of other necessities, not being available to home school.

The result has been many children at home alone supposedly learning. Nature and human development has provided for a substantial period of time before children can safely make decisions without the input of adult care takers. If it were not so, our children would be born fully capable of leaving the nest.

Even baby birds don't survive, much less thrive, being pushed from the nest too early.

Grandson Micah joined me many times to bake.

It Takes Two

When I think of the things that take at least two, it's an eye opener.

There are natural occurrences in life that tend to leave us in a solitary state. Being alone, however, is lamented in stories, songs and even poetry.

From earliest life, babies can actually become depressed when deprived of human companionship. Infants light up, coo and reach out to anyone who engages with them. They yearn to be held and talked to. In the absence of such interaction, studies show little humans can give up on life. I think we instinctively know this.

Sometimes children don't want others to know that they want to be included. Schoolmates might ignore us, or worse, bully us. Some kids react to isolation by lashing out. Others might withdraw even more. In any event, solitary existence is not the natural state of things.

On this matter, I have advised children of all ages that they might have to make the first move toward friendship. More and more little people are growing up with feelings of rejection. This can happen for various reasons even with the best-meaning caretakers. Regardless of the cause, the reality of childhood is that there are kids who are waiting for others to reach out to them first. It can be a standoff.

During my many years of teaching high school, most of the conversations I overheard throughout any day were dealing with what was happening, or more to the point, what was not happening in relationships. I believe it is safe to say that most people are hoping to not do this life alone.

The times we are in have taken a toll on relationship-making and maintaining. This mandated isolation just made an already difficult socializing issue even worse.

Children of families with multiple kids at home found that their siblings became their playmates if they were to have any. As the pandemic has worn on, people have been more creative at getting social time with their friends and colleagues. Skype and other electronic options have helped people connect, albeit not in person. Play dates can happen electronically. Meetings with varying participants are happening via various online applications.

One thing that is not happening is the making of new relationships. The numerous online dating programs have proven that getting to know someone only electronically is inadequate and even misleading. Without meeting in person, prospective companions can pretend to be anyone they choose. It is difficult to really know someone you met in an online environment.

Adults not seeking personal companions might still like to meet new people. If the only way they are exposed to persons they don't yet know is via the internet, new connections rarely happen. I have been part of virtual book studies and even organizational meetings including ones from my faith community. I notice new faces but am unable to engage in meaningful conversation.

There's the common expression, "It takes two to Tango." I don't know why needing two to dance comes to mind, but it represents all the ways human contact is important to the experience. I suppose two people could go through the motions each in their own rooms, but isn't the connection the point?

I find it interesting that sometimes animals, domesticated and wild, get it right when we who are more civilized flounder. My dog Annie constantly seeks physical contact with me. When I am sitting, she comes to me and pushes her body against my leg. She stands in this pose as long as I allow. It's almost like she is refueling by this connection. I know she thrives because of being able to touch me.

We know this to be true in our human world as well. How can we survive with less?

Siblings Micah and Ava got on each other's nerves during the confinement.

Too Close, Too Long?

Hanging out with family becoming a problem? Home-schoolers have had to work this out long ago, but for many families this pandemic-dictated, distance-learning marathon presents proximity problems, now complicated more by our unsafe air here in California.

At first those who were suddenly called on to make their homes learner-friendly have had the sometimes impossible task of providing separate, quiet spaces for each of their children.

My 7th-grade grandson Lev commented about being sequestered with his four siblings. "I wish I didn't have to be around them as much, because sometimes they get annoying. Sometimes I like to work it out by wrestling with my five-year-old brother (Micah). Usually Dad says 'wild goes outside,' but not possible with all the bad air." Having so much time together in a confined space makes for frayed nerves.

In contrast, kindergartener Micah loves having his siblings around. He wants everyone to play with him when he has any breaks from his schoolwork. If this were a normal school year he would be at school half day and the other part of the day he would be home with his two-year-old sister and either his mother or grandmother. His two brothers and sister would have been at school most of the day and not available to be his playmates. He is excited that all the kids are home.

Except for not getting to run around outside, this little guy doesn't seem as bothered by the mandate to stay at home. He does, however, really miss seeing his age mates, especially his closest friend, Rory. It had been over six months since he had seen Rory when they were recently allowed a play date.

These kids, in fact, all my younger grandkids, have had no experience being around anyone with COVID. I know that the youngest one has no idea what all the fuss is about. All he knows is how his little world has been altered.

My other set of four grandkids has a similar set of problems. The oldest, Corey, has begun virtual college and is very independent, but the three younger ones are in middle and elementary school. Fortunately, they also have a big enough house that each child can be in a quiet area for meeting with their teachers online. For the most part, there is harmony when they are offline, but occasionally tempers flare. Again, if they were able to run around outside, many conflicts could be averted.

So how are the parents of distance-learning kids doing? Neither sets of parents of all nine of these grandkids are getting the same quality of time with each other. When they are home they are overseeing their children's studies, much more than they would have if their students were in school and just bringing homework to complete.

My son and his wife have a long-established weekly date that got them out for at least a meal where they could reconnect. Given the pandemic, however, most of this time eating places weren't open. Subsequently, sometimes a date consisted of their getting takeout and eating it in their cars. Given the hazardous air of the last couple of months, however, they haven't felt safe even leaving home.

These are challenging times. Some families are seeing more of each other with varying degrees of quality time. Some families are stressed trying to keep their jobs while still providing supervision for their homebound students. Everyone seems to agree that our home lives are not business as usual. The disruption of the pandemic and fires has changed the basic operation of our lives.

We are closer than ever without necessarily being close.

Our family of 19 were a sequestered "pod" so gathering for dinner was still festive. Thanksgiving of 2020.

Dinner by Design

It takes effort to push against the compulsion to withdraw completely. Have you noticed that there are people – even friends – that you have not talked to in a long time? Just because we are ordered to not gather or to only gather in smaller groups, with social distancing and masks, we can still reach out to friends and family.

Think of the ways you used to get together. If you used to meet with a friend on a regular basis in person, try keeping that appointment by telephone, Skype, Zoom or even in person in whatever way keeps you compliant.

At this time in our area, restaurants are only open for outside dining. So do it. It is summer and we are in triple-digit weather right now, which is not conducive for eating outside. Look for places to eat that offer misters and good cover or go at a time when the weather is the most comfortable. Don't just skip meeting with friends. It requires more effort, but staying connected is so important.

Think of the psychology of no longer hanging out, even casually, with others. When we are no longer connected in a meaningful way, we are limited to our own counsel. This is the breeding ground for dark thoughts – thoughts of inadequacy, rejection, hurt feelings, paranoia, despair. I am not making this up!

I am not just talking about adults. Watch the children. In these pandemic times many are isolated in a room – sometimes their bedrooms – sitting, staring at their computers.

There is a natural pull to disconnect when the stimulus is not very intense, especially when there is a mind-numbing blue light radiating into your eyeballs. One of my granddaughters remarked that the light of the computer makes her sleepy. Indeed. Double trouble: the urge to go to sleep, which is the great disconnect, and nothing or no one to pull you back into the moment. Does anyone else think about how depressed people want to sleep a lot?

Adults have a difficult time motivating themselves to keep up their usual duties. How much more difficult is it for kids? We need to help them know how to consciously resist the desire to disengage. The more our environment presents us with mind-numbing experiences that we cannot even share with others, the more we need to work at not allowing ourselves to slide down the path of least resistance.

So, that is why I recommend intentionally planning for meet ups. Whether you are young or older, find the place to go that allows you to maintain your human connections. Don't wait for others to invite you. Nine times out of ten your friends are probably waiting for you to make the first move. That becomes a stalemate. Be brave. Reach out first. You might even find that your efforts to stay in others' lives, and they in yours, can lead to deepening your relationship.

It has been pointed out, however, that there may be resistance to accepting offers to get together. I have friends who tried to invite people and were refused. Those declining characterized themselves as being more in touch with the real problems and insinuated that my friends were oblivious and even insensitive.

Be that as it may, instead of this time of the pandemic being remembered as The Great Disconnect, let 2020 become the year of The Great Connection instead. Staying in each others' lives is a decision we need to make for our own well-being. We need others and they need us. Don't let anything keep us from being together. There are going to be troubled times with or without an actual pandemic. The other part of the human condition is that where there is a will, there is always a way.

I suggested eating with someone because breaking bread together is the traditionally best way – and most comforting – to engage one another in meaningful conversation. Let's exercise our free will and invite someone to dinner or even to the park, or to play a chess game. You get the idea. We are only limited by our imaginations on how to get together.

Human relationships are what make this life worth living. Reach out and cheer someone up and you'll find you'll feel better, too.

-C-

SCHOOL & WORK

Several of my grandchildren attend this elementary school that was like a ghost town.

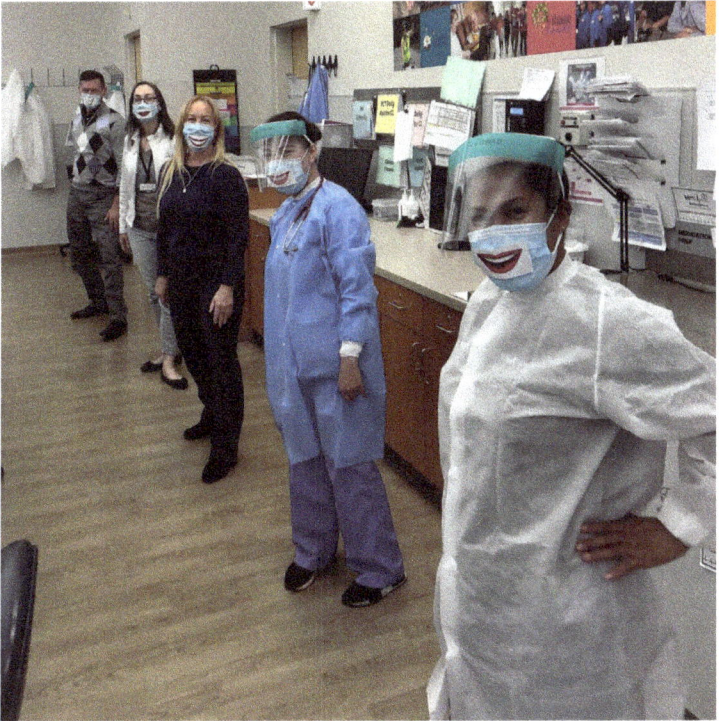

*Health care professionals were the hardest hit by the Pandemic.
My daughter-in-law Rosemary Rubinstein, RD, is the second from left.*

Jobs in Jeopardy

Many places of employment have not been able to survive the COVID restrictions on their ability to conduct business. Establishments that were offering a service necessitating the provider to be inside the "bubble" of safety of six feet were summarily shut down when the mandates began. If the business survived that period, they were then highly regulated upon re-opening.

As expected, all service industries have been very hard hit. I wouldn't have thought that this would include services such as gardening, but they too were restricted. Restaurants were high on the list of being potentially dangerous because people can't eat with their masks on.

In "normal" times, if an employer closes his doors, those who worked for him might apply for a similar job with another establishment. What we have encountered instead is that entire classes of businesses have been closed as not being "essential." Most have been gradually re-opened as authorities report fewer new corona cases, but restrictions persist including social distancing, masking and even cuts to how much of their service they could provide.

For many the wait was too long so they were compelled to shut their doors for good. Two of my favorite restaurants – both family-owned – did not survive COVID. It was eight months before I got a haircut. It was equally long before I could get a pedicure which is very essential since I am a diabetic.

Some businesses found that they could weather the storm by sending their employees home to work. Many fields, however, are almost impossible to continue conducting their kind of business strictly online.

Some new lines of work have opened up for those who can adapt. Delivery persons are in great demand. More people are ordering online everything from groceries to take-out meals. Online providers of goods, such as Amazon, have experienced a boon during this time. UPS and FedEx have grown their businesses delivering all these online-ordered goods.

What happens to a society when entire categories of jobs are eliminated or are so significantly impacted that they can no longer conduct business as usual? Historically we have experienced this kind of shift after natural disasters such as the Mount St. Helens volcano eruption of 1980 that NPR reported "seemed Apocalyptic." Hurricane Katrina in 2005 was a Category 5 hurricane that affected most of the Eastern U.S. and Eastern Canada with hundreds of deaths and 125 billion in damages. Many places of business never returned to their pre-hurricane state.

We in California continue to be hard hit by wildfires. In August of 2020 there were 367 known fires, many sparked by intense thunderstorms. California has a five-year average of almost 5,000 wildfires. Other Pacific Coast states have also experienced such fires, with Oregon hard hit in July 2020, the cause reported as high winds and dry weather.

Some horrendous man-made disasters – actually terrorist attacks – have had the effect of stopping us in our tracks. We still ask, "Where were you when the Towers went down?" Life as we knew it changed radically that day.

Rarely do we encounter such magnitude of worldwide effects from a single event, with the possible exception of the World Wars and the Great Depression, of course. This pandemic has impacted the workforce globally. After such widespread tragedies, life never really goes back to where it was before.

Sometimes the changes can be ultimately good, shaking the status quo, such as when women realized their value as workers while the men were fighting in the great wars. Some workers have used this opportunity to get more education – virtually – to be better prepared to compete for jobs.

Maybe another positive outcome is that we had been putting too much stock in workers having to leave home to do their line of work. Remote working has had many obvious benefits. Sometimes it takes catastrophe for us to shift our thinking, daring to believe what we are used to may not be the best solution for moving forward.

I would never want to minimize the pain of tragedy experienced by so many, but as we pull ourselves out of the debris, there are lessons learned that can better the way we do business. What we each do to make our living is important to us, while benefitting society as a whole.

The expression comes to mind, "It takes a village." These words are usually spoken to help us realize that raising children takes a community. The same can be said for our line of work. Every job is providing a vital part of the total workings of our society. We may have to adapt and shift and perhaps even change fields, but what we do is needed.

Your job – no matter how menial or lofty you might think it is – is an important part of the fabric of our lives.

No one is dispensable.

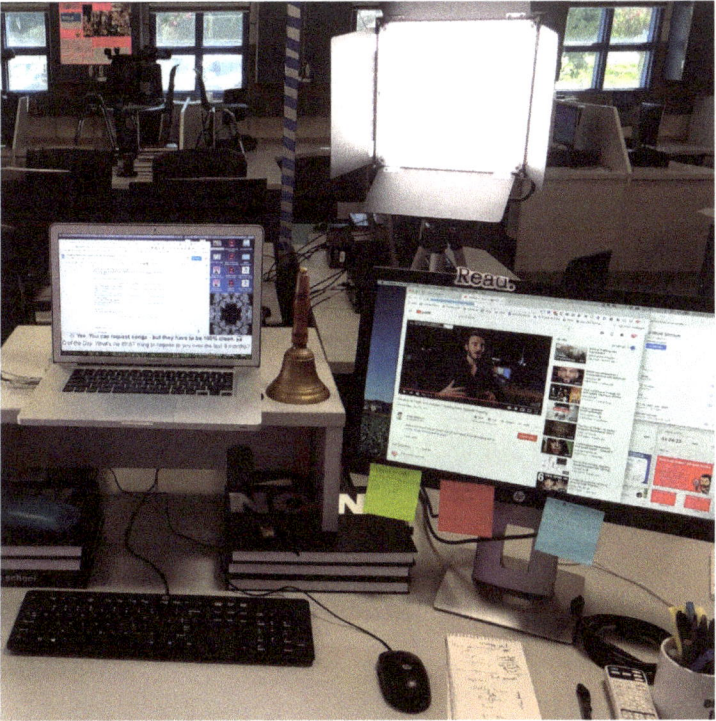

Son Joshua's Zoom setup to teach journalism, yearbook and photojournalism.

Technology Explosion

In my 40 years of teaching I saw many changes in technology, but never at the fast pace of this year. Adapting to the rapid advances in various technologies to allow for distance learning as well as businesses sending their workers home to work has made a huge impact on our society. Since in recent years there has been a surge in people working at home, the business world has adapted more seamlessly to the new restrictions than our school systems.

The youngest of distance learners has had to become very computer savvy. Even my kindergarten grandson Micah commented, "I am going to be a big computer guy by next year." And he is correct. It is dizzying to see a five-year-old navigate the various applications used to present his lessons from school to home.

In my former teaching field of publications and journalism I used more technology than most teachers. In the beginning I had the most basic personal computers – which happened to be Apples – for my journalists to use to produce the school newspaper. They word-processed all stories and our editors used a desktop publishing application to layout the pages before printing out and delivering them to the publisher.

As the years progressed we graduated to submitting our pages completely by computer, which by that time were several generations newer. We were submitting digital photos, no longer needing to develop and print out our photographs. My exposure to computer technology has been much more than most.

Up to this last year, teachers have had varying needs to know technology. Some subjects required almost no use of technology except that students word process their work. Teachers did not rely on technology beyond turning on a movie or video in the classroom. The most difficult technology demand was assisting students to make classroom presentations via computers.

Enter the coronavirus. All education became distance learning. Teachers and students alike had to depend on their ability to learn enough about the required technology to function solely online.

Educators had to scurry to figure out how to present their subjects to their students electronically. School districts spent massive amounts of money providing every student a chrome book – the name given to small laptops. Systems were developed for parents to pick up needed materials outside of school offices. Videos were produced to help families understand the new delivery of lessons. Suddenly, every teacher had to master many levels of technology.

And then there's the students. Today's youth are used to most computer and television viewing to be very passive, computer games notwithstanding. I am sitting with one of my fifth grade grandkids, Hannah, as I am writing this. Her teacher is instructing on subtracting decimals. The kids all have workbooks in front of them to follow along as the teacher explains the concept.

I watch as Hannah's eyes glaze over, time and again. She has even lined up the chairs in the dining room – which is her "classroom" workspace – so she can slip down into a reclining position every few minutes. I encourage her to get up and run around or do jumping jacks to get some oxygen to the brain. I suggest a snack.

At this writing – in mid-September 2020 – the school systems in our area have had varying plans for reopening schools. My teacher-son's school district has proposed a hybrid school opening next Monday whereby the students will attend live classes every other day and be required to complete work independently on the off days.

There were many flaws in this proposal, so his school chose to instead offer a 4-by-4 program where these teens get a full year of credit in four courses each semester. The delivery is still, however, shortened days so no lunch is offered and students are in class working on their chrome books. Some teachers are continuing distance learning for families desiring it.

The local elementary and middle schools are planning to begin a hybrid system in November, which affects six of my grandkids. They first offered for students to spend half a day in live classes and then be home completing assignments the other half without teacher help as they will be instructing the other half of the student population. The district settled on a shortened school day that would not include lunch, sending students home with much more homework than they had with regular school.

I think we are all hoping that educators will use their newly acquired skills in technology to create tutorials for their students to access when these kids are on their own.

But also a problem is considering the dilemma from the teachers' standpoint. When exactly would they have the time to create such interventions? They will be fulfilling their contractual obligations by just teaching full time every day. They have been pushed to deliver over and above to bridge the gap posed by distance learning and to distill their subject matter so that it is accessible to children on computers. They are not even using live textbooks for fear of spreading the virus so teachers are having to re-create the wheel with technology. This despite us learning early on that the virus is not long viable or transmissible on surfaces.

Without our modern technology this pandemic would have shut down education in most of the world. We have been able to redeem the situation from being a total loss, but even our newfound expertise can't solve everything and possibly presents a new set of problems.

I do have concerns that the teaching field may not look as enticing as a career. It's one thing for a teacher to go to college to study a desired field. It is another to also have to become expert in providing that education remotely.

When I think of how technology has evolved over my lifetime, I know I have not been able to keep up. For the most part, however, these advances have come about slowly with occasional spurts. During this pandemic the need for more superior uses has been an explosion.

Once the dust settles, if we ever get back to even a new normal, we will have to re-evaluate how these rapid changes have impacted our everyday lives. It's becoming apparent that we can never return to our pre-high tech days. I do have concerns that the bar has been raised so high.

Our way of life depends on how well we adapt as a people.

I helped my children's families a couple of times a week supervising distance learning. On this day my grandson Micah and I took our class outside. The glasses are just to offset the damaging blue light of the computer.

Distance Learning during COVID

What a dilemma. Students have to study their lessons. With schools being surprised with learning online instead of in person, those first three months of the pandemic, completing the 2020 school year became a hastily-concocted hodgepodge of lessons. Educators and learners were equally caught off guard. Most teachers sent instructional videos that were not interactive. It was difficult for the students to engage.

By the beginning of the school year 2020-2021, educators were offering live classes online, intermixed with breakout sessions and some video instruction. Still students report it is easy to get behind and many do. It is even possible for these young students to completely tune out major assignments, doing only those lessons that are live each day. Sometimes the lengthy projects have not been broken down into what the child should be doing daily, so it has not been uncommon for parents to find out their child has put off a project for several weeks. I have seen several of my grandkids caught in this dilemma. I hear it is a widespread problem.

This has been the plight of public schools while some of the alternative schools – such as the charters – having already employed distance learning as part of their regular curriculum found the transition less troublesome. Even they, however, were not expecting all of the lessons to be online, students not being allowed to attend school at all. These institutions also have contracts with the parents as co-teachers, so they were assured that at least one adult would be home with the suddenly-sequestered students.

In contrast, so-called comprehensive schools, private and public, had two problems continuing online. First, and foremost, there was no guarantee that there would be an adult in all the homes, as previously discussed.

The second issue is whether the curriculum usually delivered in an active, live classroom can be adapted to only online. Some subjects lend themselves better to this change. The 3 R's – "reading, writing and 'rithmetic" – work pretty well for distance learning.

Even in these courses, however, there comes the moment in any class where student interaction is important. The teachers are attempting to organize small groups into breakout sessions. In a classroom this would be where the teacher would circulate, fielding questions and keeping everyone on task. Teachers cannot see what is going on in another breakout room as they circulate electronically. Therefore no one is surprised to find that some students get up to mischief within these rooms.

Today I witnessed a break out room incident that got out of hand. A couple of the fifth-grade boys started "spamming." My granddaughter informed me that this is when a person just starts typing nonsense – or worse – to the class on their computers. One student posted a spinning wheel that was very distracting. Meanwhile the students are instructed to not close their computers. I had my granddaughter turn her computer screen away and turn off the sound. The teacher admonished the students behaving badly when she pulled all the kids back into the virtual classroom.

Next week, on Election Day, our county has called for the schools to be reopened. All but TK – transitional kindergarten – and kindergarteners will be masked. Some parents have chosen to have their children continue distance learning. Their absence from the classrooms will help the schools maintain social distancing for their masked students. Schools are allowing live classes for only five hours a day, which leaves out some subjects such as PE and art, which will continue to be offered online. This is to be the plan until this school year ends. Unless there is another surge in COVID.

All in all, parents and educators are expressing real concerns for what has been lost. Everyone agrees that at very least all children's education has been seriously interrupted. In addition, many have become passive learners. A few have even used the online platform as their stage for distracting others at a whole new level, without benefit of immediate consequences.

There were some obvious gains from our children experiencing distance learning. Even though this generation already boasted computer savvy way beyond that of their parents, they have exceeded their own pre-corona levels. In fact, which is actually a negative, many of the children have figured out how to tune out their teachers by simultaneously operating other technology apps such as games or being on YouTube. Otherwise, some children seemed to excel at using technology for their schooling. These are probably the ones whose parents will have them continue online.

A "mixed" review coming from lessons being online is that parents are getting to see what teachers are saying to their classes. This week I observed a Science/Math teacher in middle school presenting a lesson on hand washing – due to COVID. She presented her students with an artist's rendering of "facts" on how long the virus could live on surfaces. My grandson in the class noted that she claimed the virus could live up to three days. He "privately chatted" with her and countered the claim with what his father had told him, ostensibly that the virus could only last a few minutes on surfaces at best. The teacher chatted back that he was wrong.

She continued on, spontaneously adding to the message, by telling these sixth graders that the place people are the most likely to get the virus is in church. My grandson again chatted to the teacher that he attends worship service twice a month. The teacher responded that he was breaking the law. Incidentally, the law at that moment was not forbidding faith communities to meet, but attendance was severely restricted in numbers and activities.

I was incensed. I asked my grandson to tell the teacher that the next chat was from his grandmother. I told her that pushing personal political positions had no place in the curriculum. I said that there was significant evidence that ran counter to what she was teaching. We watched her read the private chat and she immediately told the class that the session was over and she shut it down.

Having been a teacher myself for over 40 years, I know that teachers teach as much who they are as the content they are delivering. I know we are tempted to share our own convictions with our charges, but we must resist as they are very impressionable, especially when the information is coming from a teacher for whom they have a lot of respect. Nuf said.

The task is before us all. How do we pull kids back to a level of learning that will prepare them for the next year? Will we have to remediate the subsequent grades to give space for students to catch up, perhaps filling in the obvious gaps in their learning? Does this effect ripple upward indefinitely? Can we come back to a normal learning curve?

Everyone is looking at what this year has brought as having displaced our normal routines. We talk of a New Normal. What will it be for education? At very least we must incorporate more user-friendly computer programs because today's students have become very savvy about working online, but also because we don't know if we might have to resort to distance learning again. "Be Prepared" must be the motto.

We also know that we have the added responsibility of rekindling passion for learning in our upcoming generation. The to-be-expected passivity of our kids must be addressed. If teachers ever realized that what they present is a "dog and pony" show, they will have to step it up a few notches to reign in our COVID kids. Learning, by definition, requires personal engagement.

How we will re-engage today's distant youth will be the topic of conversation for some time to come. Let's get up close and personal.

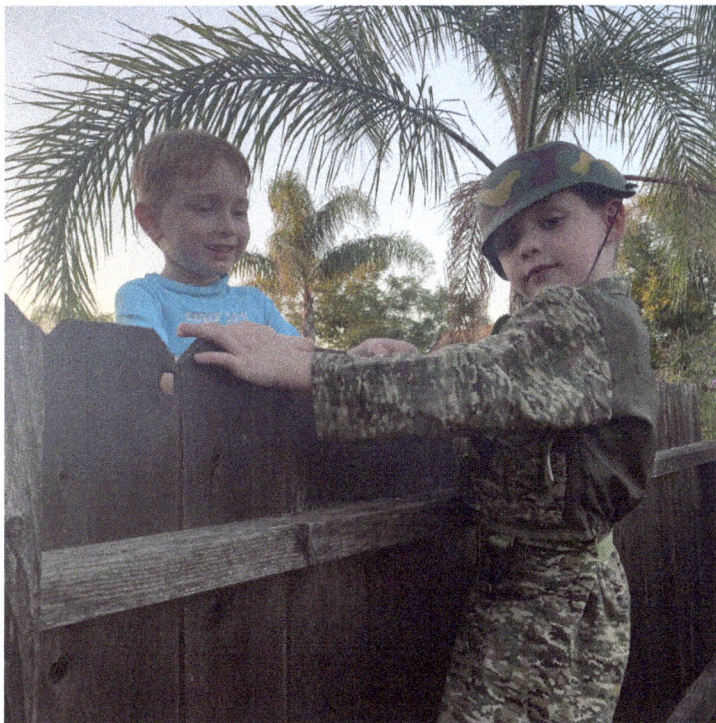

Micah and Rory were always together until COVID. Since Rory lives next door to Micah's Uncle Mike and Aunt Sarah, he sometimes got to reconnect over the fence. Photo provided by Rory's mother, Jen Worth.

Micah and Rory

These two little guys were inseparable. They knew each other before TK started in the fall of 2019. Rory's family lives next door to Micah's aunt and uncle's family. Any time Micah visited his cousins, he would try to get time with Rory.

A couple of times a week, as Micah's grandmother, I would be the one to take Micah and his siblings to school. Any time they got there early these two friends were running around, laughing and playing. On one occasion they got an idea to strap themselves to a lamppost by the TK classroom door. Rory's dad and I had a few moments of frustration making sure they got free quickly to be on time for class. The boys were never worried and giggled through the whole scene.

Last year Micah and Rory were in TK class together. They got to sit by each other until the teacher told them they chatted too much. She separated them. Micah said it was really hard to have his friend across the room. They didn't get to be together except at recess.

By February of this school year the coronavirus was wreaking havoc worldwide. It affected everyone, especially the schools. Health officials were recommending that children and teachers be sent home for an extended spring break. Within a week the decision to close all schools swept our country.

Rory and Micah had not been able to see each other during all this time due to the mandated "sequestering in place" and restrictions that eliminated gatherings. Micah was often visiting just next door to Rory's house at his cousins' house, but still unable to see Rory. Once I was there when Micah's dad lifted him up to see over the fence into Rory's yard. It was a magical momentary reconnection.

The 2020-2021 school year began with only distance learning allowed in California. As it happens, when kindergarten classes were organized, Rory and Micah were put in the same class again but at different times such that they are in class only one of the three hours together. None of the children, however, have been able to have private conversations. The teacher keeps them muted on their chrome books except to respond to her questions, in which case they raise their hands and she shuffles through the several "pages" of Zoom students to determine who she will call on.

Kindergarten's greatest lesson is for children to experience how to interact with each other in a learning environment. Frankly, once they get basic number concepts and the alphabet and its accompanying sounds, the only "content" is to learn some basic math functions and practice the fluidity of reading while building vocabulary.

Socializing is one of the major purposes for this class. Kindergarteners across this country have missed a vital part of their readiness for continued learning. IF schools are open next year, the expectation is for these youngsters to be classroom-ready. They won't have had the opportunity to hang out and enjoy social interaction except for brief recesses. Will they be sufficiently socialized for entering first grade?

Will there be a lasting negative impact on these learners? Only time will tell, but common sense informs us that this was a developmental loss, not just a gap from a curricular subject that a student might discover in future lessons. It's deeper than whether my grandson Micah and his friend Rory can maintain a meaningful relationship. It's about a whole generation of kindergarteners experiencing disconnect when they developmentally needed the opposite.

We can only hope that first grade teachers across our nation can bridge the gap by allowing for their next year's students to have more time socializing. If not, I'm afraid these little people will be craving contact when the expectation is for them to be fully prepared to learn.

These youngsters could misbehave in ways misinterpreted as discipline problems when all they need is time to catch up on forming friendships.

Five of my grandkids – Eitan, Lev, baby Ava, mom Rosemary and Eliana returning from biking to picnic at the local park. With limited access to their own friends they have their siblings as playmates. The parents schedule them for outdoor activities.

The New Couch Potatoes

We have all had our concerns about people who spend too much time sitting, usually playing games or watching TV. This behavior is usually combined with snacking – a recipe for an unhealthy life.

Many parents continue to work to limit their children's exposure to electronic devices. Children are encouraged to get outside or just read or have other "unplugged" fun.

Prior to this pandemic, during school season students typically came home and ran straight to their computers or televisions. I know some parents limit their children's exposure to the mind numbing and blue light of "technology." Optical sales have risen to the occasion by offering glasses – with or without prescription – that deflect the blue light, but they are not a match for the massive increase in screen time of our next generation.

The dilemma with the current mandated distance learning is that children are on computers for a minimum of six hours, five times a week. I have heard my grandchildren trying to negotiate with their parents for additional time playing games on their devices after their schoolwork is completed. Parents are concerned that their kids should get away from the screen completely once their online classes are over.

That makes for a bunch of unhappy children at odds with their parents. The alternative scenario is that some children are not limited in their use of electronic devices after school so are getting excessive exposure.

We, as a society, have to share concerns of the impact of so much technology on eyes and minds. A psychological side effect of so much use of electronic devices is that users tend to get detached and disconnected. We can hope neither of these effects has a far-reaching impact on our society.

The other issue that was already plaguing America is that inactive people – i.e. persons in front of screens – tend toward grazing. If we were cows, this would not be a problem. When animals graze, it is on herbs and grasses. If people are inclined to forage, they need to be sure that they are eating similar foods to that of bovine critters.

We tend to eat whatever is in front of us. With all our children couch-bound, there is more unconscious eating. Parents can hit this problem head on by being very conscious of what snacks they put out for their home-bound students. Even if children are eating more, it could be healthy foods rather than the alluring, adulter-ated, addictive junk food.

And then there is the problem of increased inactivity. California kids have had the added restriction of hav-ing so much bad air that they are not allowed outside to play during their scheduled recesses, nor before and after school. Six of my grandchildren were into the rou-tine of riding their bicycles to and from school before this pandemic hit.

Exercise has to be carefully planned for our kids. Some families have begun working out together. With gyms being closed, I have noticed more home gyms springing up in garages. Even if there are increased planned trips to parks or other outdoor recreation venues, home exercising can go a long way to helping our kids get fit. As long as the weather holds and clean air persists, kids can bicycle or use their scooters and skateboards every day. Let's get them off the couches and moving.

Lack of exercise and consuming increasing amounts of fattening snack foods could prove disastrous deter-rents to the overall health of our future adults. Parents can, however, turn things around by intentional plan-ning.

My youngest grandson literally asks for lettuce to snack on. Granted, his mother is a Registered Dietitian who makes sure all her family realizes how important veggies are to every meal or snack. Just increasing veg-etable intake alone can improve overall health.

There is a lot at stake. The threat is real. We must be proactive to save our kids. Our nation is only as healthy as our next generation.

-D-

BIRTH & DEATH

Granddaughter Eliana's 8th grade graduation to high school
was confined to their house. Micah, Ava, Eliana, Lev, Eitan Rubinstein.

The Uncelebrations

These times of social distancing and limited gatherings are especially difficult in the events in our lives that mark rites of passage. Our family celebrates birthdays monthly. We all joke about our own "March Madness" as we have eight birthdays to celebrate in this spring month alone.

The sequestering of this pandemic began in March, pushing our March birthdays into the background. As many as dared got together, but the joy was dampened.

There were some age milestones in our family this year, as almost every year. Three of my grandkids hit double digits! Two officially hit age 12 and are on the verge of teenagedom. On the youngest end of the spectrum my son and daughter-in-law's little foster baby turned two.

There were five family school benchmarks at the close of school year 2020. My TK grandson moved into kindergarten, two grandkids graduated elementary and began middle school, one began high school and another began college. The two oldest grandkids each got into their own apartments as they continued to work and attend college.

That all may sound very fluid, but it was quite the contrary. All ten of my school-age grandkids were sent home to finish the last few months of the school year, college included. By the time they completed this school year, they each were ready for congratulations. We would have been showering them with well wishes any other year, but instead there were some "drive by" acknowledgments of birthdays and educational accomplishments in our circle of family and friends. And, lest I forget, most graduates were given congratulatory signs for their front lawns. Spectacular. Not.

The forced isolation of COVID hit every kind of life cycle event. Weddings were planned for but thwarted by venues closing, clergy unavailable, participants and well-wishers being confined to quarters. When nuptials did happen, they were limited to just a few celebrants. Even the officiants tended to keep their distance from the wedding couple. I wonder how they managed "the kiss"?

Weddings could be simplified and postponed, but there are some events that cannot be put off. Only time will tell, but there seems to be a record number of pregnant women this year, at least in the U. S. Babies will be born at their appointed times. The difficulty has been in there being many restrictions on even the number of participants at the event. All celebrations surrounding this moment of new life entering the world have been constricted.

Finally, those who are leaving this world, their bodies having run each's own personal race, are transitioning on a sad silent note. Bodies will be buried, but those hoping to celebrate their deceased loved ones are unable to do so in person.

I suspect we take celebrating these life cycle events for granted. It is not until we cannot fully express our emotions publicly that we realize what we have lost. "Hello" and "Goodbye" and all the expressions of "Well done" in between are essential for our society to be in balance. Without them, life seems to be off kilter.

*My daughter, Sarah, was a last-minute officiate at
a friend's wedding in an open-air venue with limited guests.*

Nuptial Nightmare

If there is one day in most people's lives they dream would go smoothly, it would have to be their wedding day. These are trying times for tying the knot.

You might ask, what could go wrong? Well, actually, quite a few things.

First, as I mentioned earlier, there are many venues shut down either due to COVID restrictions or our hazardous air days from our fires in northern California.

With the reportedly unpredictable coronavirus, government officials have allowed for some openings of gathering places, only to withdraw permission days later. So if the bride and groom are able to secure a place, there is the added angst that their chosen site could be closed at the last moment.

Second, ministers and other wedding officiants are not always available due to our guarded conditions. I know of a couple who was trying to arrange their wedding. For both of them it was a second marriage, so they were content to have it be simpler. Their most important consideration was to find a time and place that worked for the minister. This couple had ties to spiritual communities in both southern and northern California.

They were hoping to have their ceremony in northern California where they both reside. Their local minister was hesitant to "do a wedding." He wanted to spend time counseling the couple prior to officiating a ceremony, especially since both participants had been married previously and divorced, and at least one of them was new to this minister's community. Given COVID constraints, it became impossible to have in-person counseling sessions. Scheduling either Skype or Zoom was equally difficult.

The couple thought they would drive south and have their former minister officiate. Given the complications of their lives – with jobs and three children between them – taking the eight-hour drive was determined to be impossible. They knew that either of their possible locations would restrict the number of participants, so they had to let go of the desire to celebrate with loved ones.

After weeks of anguishing, this couple decided to have a civil wedding. They went before a magistrate for their nuptials where they were not allowed to have any of their friends and family present. This was certainly not the hoped-for ceremony.

Another wedding that affects our family will be attended by my daughter and her husband. The wedding couple has had similar concerns securing a venue and an officiant and limiting their guest list to fit COVID. My daughter just told me yesterday that the person who was to marry them was no longer able to attend. The bride – a work colleague of my daughter's for over ten years – asked my daughter if she would be willing to take over as the officiant. They know she is not a minister, but neither the bride nor groom consider themselves to be religious.

Fortunately, the wedding couple was able to give my daughter several weeks' notice. She ordered a license online to conduct weddings and received it days before the scheduled nuptials. What she had planned to wear to the wedding changed knowing that she was to lead the ceremony. Yesterday she was able to find a dress that doubles as suitable for a person who is officiating as well as being a celebrant.

That's what it is like during these times. Everyone has had to go to at least Plan B, sometimes Plan C. There are some who have even postponed their nuptials until both the virus and the fires are no longer a threat.

This year being a June bride is proving undoable. In our state, most weddings are being planned for the winter when we typically will have had some cleansing rains. The fires could be under control, but there are still no guarantees that the COVID pandemic will have run its course. What a nightmare!

Wedding day dreams are dashed. It is memorable, but not what was imagined.

Foster baby – and creative fashionista – Ava came to my son Joshua and wife Rosie's family as a two-month-old and was about to be fully adopted when COVID struck. All courts were closed except for emergencies. It wasn't until February 24th, 2021 that the adoption was finalized to the family's joy.

Babies Born in Isolation

Life goes on. So much of nature is already set in its natural process. These events can't be stopped or put on hold when a pandemic hits. Obviously childbirth is one. What has changed, however, is how families deal with this very special event.

Friends of mine were happily expecting the birth of their first child. Every aspect of this event was impacted. The momma would normally have been part of a birthing class. During this time the class was not even available most of the time. Whatever this expectant mom needed to know about the process of the pregnancy and how to be prepared for the birthing process had to be learned online.

I think expectant parents get much more from being in a live class with other soon-to-be mommies and daddies. This is the place where advice flows freely, especially from couples that have had other children. It is fair to say that this group is as much for encouragement as to learn specific birthing techniques. That pivotal part is missing.

I attended the baby shower for my friend. It was held in one of her friend's homes in the town where they all live. Great care was taken by the hostess to provide for social distancing, masking and food preparation. A masked child met guests at the door offering each a handmade cloth mask to put on and keep.

Tables were set up in the large living space. Participants were encouraged to place themselves six feet from someone not in their immediate family. Some of the games traditionally played at showers were missing if they required guests to be in close proximity to each other. The lunch provided consisted of individual items that would not require handling.

After several games were enjoyed and prizes distributed, cupcakes were served. The hostess felt it was safer to not have the traditional cake, but offer cupcakes so there would not be any potential for people to touch anything but their own dessert. Upon leaving, several ladies hugged but many others did the pandemic elbow bump.

Some of the key persons who would have come to this shower – such as the parents of the prospective mother and father – were prevented from attending as they live too far away and air travel was prohibited. I was able to drive to the shower from my home which is over an hour away. This couple has ties in my community and also has many friends and other family in the town where they reside.

Our community wanted to also throw them a baby shower, but most of the persons who would have attended were not comfortable being in a meeting with more than ten persons. That was the mandate for our town at the time. The expectant parents had provided a baby registry whereby well-wishers could choose gifts online and have them sent to the parents.

As time grew closer, my friends worked on preparing to receive their new little one. Doctor's appointments were attended since a physical exam for the mom was needed as the time for delivery drew close. The husband was allowed to attend the birth, but with the corona rule of only one person helping the mom, no one else could attend. I know how important it was for my daughters to have me and a friend at their deliveries. Attending a life cycle event cannot be retrieved once lost.

This mommy's delivery was longer than she anticipated, but their baby boy joined the family only two weeks later than expected. These Jewish parents had one more covenantal event for this baby – a brit milah, or rite of circumcision. A mohel – a person trained to perform this procedure and also conduct the liturgical parts of the ceremony – was contacted but opted not to attend due to concerns of getting exposed to corona. Instead, the parents made an appointment with a pediatrician, arranged for a rabbi to attend, and were able to complete the mitzvah on the traditional eighth day, minus the community celebration.

The baby is a few weeks old at this writing. The dad had three weeks paternity leave and has returned to work. The new mommy has a few friends and family around, but not the grandparents who can't fly yet.

In future years when this event is revisited in pictures, people will note the absence of the community enveloping this new little family. I am hoping that little Jonathan will realize the missing people are an anomaly for this life-cycle celebration – a time of great hardship that lasted a short time.

Heaven forbid that such distancing becomes the "New Normal." Celebrating new life is a foundation of our society.

Subdued graduation celebration for my grandson Corey finishing high school.
All graduates were assigned a "distanced" time to show up to get their video filmed
at their school. Mom Sarah, the graduate, Corey's fiance Sarai and dad Michael.

If a graduate can't cross the stage...

...did he really graduate? Not only did 2020 graduates
– from kindergarten to college – not get to have ceremonies marking this great achievement, they had not been
in a live classroom for several months.

Our grandson Corey completed high school. When
a child reaches this time, this rite of passage, there
should be fanfare. Our family did all we could to make
our graduate feel appreciated for his culmination of 12
years of study. It is a monumental accomplishment and

a gateway to the rest of his life. Combined with the high school graduate's age – usually being 18 – they have officially entered adulthood. Balloons! Bells! Whistles! Wooohoooo...

Instead, my grandson was sent a video of a graduation speech for his school's graduating class. He was invited to go to the school and get a socially distanced turn walking across the stage. This was also videoed for the families. An appropriate-to-the-pandemic number of our family gathered in his family's living room to watch his videos. We cheered and screamed. He was asked by his parents to put on his cap and gown for us. He was embarrassed but complied. Anticlimactic.

He and his fellow seniors had been given a chance to pick up their yearbooks prior to the end of the school year, but there was no opportunity to have a yearbook-signing event. This is historically the last time most of these fellow travelers will all be together. How many of us have that annual of the year we graduated? I find a lot of enjoyment re-reading what friends and even teachers had to say to me at that time. Irretrievable loss.

And a note about the yearbook itself, the staff that produced it had a difficult time completing the book with the school closures. Not only were they not in class working to finish the publication, but many of the activities that would have been put in the book never happened. This graduating class has had much of their last year of high school undocumented. Disappointing.

High school seniors have been coached by family and school as to deciding what that next step in their lives might be. They might choose college or going to work right away or attending a trade school or even taking time off, but everyone agrees that finishing high school is a launch pad for the rest of their lives. This year's graduates, rather than feeling like spaceships ready to blast off, say they felt more like sparklers that fizzled out. Fzzzzzz.

Our high school graduate silently slid into junior college this term. No group orientation. No tour of the campus. No clamor. No camaraderie in the Commons. No quad to hang out with fellow students. No labs. No classrooms. Only what can be presented virtually exists for these matriculated college students. No one knows how long this will be the case. The prediction is that this entire school year – from kindergarten to college – will be in the Cloud. Disconnect.

Our family's other students who completed programs were affected less dramatically, but not being able to celebrate ending a segment of their learning took away a bit of the sense of accomplishment. We are a people who like benchmarks, milestones, turning points – all of which signal a job well done with a nod to the next challenge ahead.

I have a granddaughter who ended middle school, heading to her first year of high school. Their school gave each graduate a sign to put on their front lawns to proclaim their graduation. As a family, we didn't really have a graduation party for her. We acknowledged this accomplishment with gifts and accolades, but no gathering of her fellow graduates was allowed. This age group takes their very breaths from friendships. All were affected by not being able to share this moment. Deflating.

The school arranged a parade of teachers in their cars that circulated throughout the graduates' neighborhoods. There had been several of these caravans during the months of no live classes to encourage the distance learners. It was very festive, but in my mind I am contrasting this experience with a very celebrated middle school graduation of a grandson just a few years earlier. Impersonal.

We had two students completing elementary and moving on to middle school. In years past there would have been a school graduation ceremony. This year, of course, there was no such fanfare. They, too, received lawn signs signifying their completion. The kids left them up all summer. There is something very special about moving from elementary to secondary.

These kids have been as much as five years older than some of the children on their elementary campus. They have been the "big brothers" and "big sisters," spending time in the lower grades helping younger learners. They have matured so much in their assistants' roles. They are the esteemed resident scholars. Proud.

Now as they move on, they have to be reconciled to being the youngest on their new campus. Esteemed they are not. They will be the ones needing help. Sadly, they won't get to benefit from the older kids on their new campus teaming up with them. They haven't even had a tour of the middle school campus. They have only seen their new teachers online. Virtual.

So, where does all this virtual graduation leave us? Milestones not being fully embraced can affect morale and perhaps devalue the educational process. I know that any of these unsung achievements can affect our learners. But also, every part of what we have developed as important content is meant to be fully experienced. Moving from a lower – preparatory – level to a higher one is a major step that should not be minimized regardless of the dictates of society.

Our society still values education. We care very much that our kids hone skills to secure knowledge to ultimately acquire wisdom. The educational system in this country has made quality education its highest priority since the 20th century.

We realize as a people that as goes the educational

system, so goes the country. We are educating not just the future voters, but our future workers and leaders in every aspect of life.

Let's applaud their achievements even more during COVID. Our children need to know we understand how difficult it has been. For one to overcome in diversity is the most amazing accomplishment. Congratulations!

Debby Aaker

Jan 05, 1951 - Oct 07, 2020

*We lived by the Aakers outside of Santa Fe, New Mexico,
but knew each other through mutual friends and believers.
They were lifelong friends. We said goodbye to Debbie via a Zoom funeral.*

Silent Sendoff

No one wants to die alone. Our national response to this pandemic is to make it probable that anyone dying these days – whether from corona or other causes – will not be allowed to have loved ones present when it's time.

When COVID 19 began – even before it carried that name – health officials agreed that the most vulnerable among us were the elderly and persons with otherwise compromised health. Logic told us that we would probably be losing a number of our most at-risk citizens. Statistics have proven this to be correct.

In the beginning of this crisis, health care facilities did not allow anyone to enter when another had to be hospitalized unless they were too ill or unable to speak for themselves.

When elderly patients in care facilities became ill with corona, the decision was made to keep them in their nursing homes rather than transferring them to a hospital. This decision presented a two-fold problem. The first obvious issue is that more highly vulnerable residents would be exposed to corona and thus were more likely to become infected. Caretakers in these facilities are statistically stretched to deal with the routine geriatric needs of their charges. The sudden influx of seriously ill residents could and did overwhelm the infrastructure.

Second, nursing facilities usually have only one doctor providing oversight on all the resident's needs. Medical staff was not significantly increased to deal with the specialized needs of the corona-infected elderly. Accordingly, these patients were afforded a sub-standard level of medical intervention. The predictable – and thus avoidable – outcome was that large numbers of our elderly in nursing homes did not survive corona, and for the most part their passing was not attended by personal loved ones.

There are still a good number of older Americans who live with family or live alone. Those who became infected and were living with family fared better than their nursing home counterparts. Those living alone ended up in hospitals, but some were sent to convalesce – or die – in nursing homes.

My late father's younger sister – and only living sibling – had two momentous occasions during this year.

Aunt Peggy turned 94 years old and she went to be with her Lord. She lived in her own home in east Texas, close to her only son and the widower of her daughter and his new wife. They have all remained very close in her life. My oldest sister and her son and family live in the same town. There was opportunity for interaction until COVID hit.

Aunt Peggy has always presented a strong front. She was thankfully in charge of her faculties and could take pretty good care of herself, but she has always been very social. When family and friends could not visit as much, it had to have affected her. It seems to me that after COVID hit, I was getting more frequent reports of my aunt's health failing. She did not contract corona, per se, but it isn't a stretch to say that the decision to keep people apart would have affected her. Up until that time she was also still driving to small events and taking care of her own errands.

The restricted contact prohibiting celebrating her birthday was not as painful as not being able to be with more loved ones as she passed. She had been transferred to a hospital and could only have one visitor at a time.

Since her death, the family has not been able to organize a commemoration of her life. Most of the family live hundreds of miles away, some – myself included – several states away. Restrictions on air travel would have to be lifted for much of the family to come. We have postponed the memorial indefinitely, waiting for when the pandemic lifts.

In the meantime, there are also restrictions on having funerals or memorial services. One of my longest-standing friends, Debbie, passed away earlier this month from a non-corona related condition. There was a graveside service in Colorado Springs where she and her husband Don resided. The service was attended live by about 20 mourners, but was viewed by many others on Zoom.

Some of her lifetime friends, and mine, live as far away as Israel and were "attending" online, as was I from California. Even though it was good to see the faces of friends I have not seen in a long time, it felt empty. I saw them but we couldn't engage with each other. I sent a personal "chat" message to my Israeli friends, but that was the extent of the socializing. When we would have been consoling each other after the ceremony, the video service that provided the Zoom immediately disconnected us.

There is a great sense of emptiness. Undone ceremony. Undone consolation. As a society, we are comforted by gathering together to send our loved ones home. In the absence of a funeral or memorial – even with an online substitute – it feels so unfinished.

Because it is this age group that has been the hardest hit by the pandemic, this scene is being repeated all around the world. I see from the media that areas such as New York City have so many deaths that they cannot keep up with the burials, much less allowing send-offs.

So we leave this world with no fanfare, not surrounded by those we love, and they are scattered around the world instead of in each other's presence being consoled. We can only hope this is not a new normal. We can hope this too will pass.

Until then, we virtually see our loved ones off with the heaviness of there being unfinished business.

-E-

HEARTH & HOME

*On a bird's scale of 6 inches for 6 feet,
even the birds are social distancing.*

Photo by Thiago Japyassu

Families like my son's lived for packages. Actual shopping was close to impossible. Eitan, Eliana holding Micah, dad Joshua holding Ava, Lev with an attitude. Rosie was taking the picture.

Zoom View

We had already become a disconnected, isolated society before corona hit. We might all have different theories on how this came to be, but we tend to agree it is true.

To clarify, we are not disconnected from people in general, but rather we are connected in very small circles, usually online. We even depend on others to inform us about world and local conditions. Most of us get our information from the media. Even research on sensitive topics is trusted to what can be found online. In that sense, we are comfortable letting others do our legwork for us. Do we realize they are also doing our thinking for us?

When I taught high school English classes, an important part of the curriculum was to show students how to do authentic research. We talked about verifiable and reputable sources and tracing our information from the original source rather than recaps by others. We talked about which types of sources were more reliable – i.e., books versus magazines, newspapers and newscasts.

I retired over ten years ago, and already students were using every type of online source as research. Rarely did they go back to lengthy works of the persons most reputable in the field. Something vital was lost when this transition was accepted. The information gathered is sketchy at best.

Adults tend to choose their media based on those that see life as they do. Whatever political or philosophical direction a person leans, there are accommodating materials and broadcasts that affirm their beliefs or suspicions. Politicians not only realize this, they work it to their advantage.

What this has led to is information being disseminated from a bird's eye view. Newsworthy occurrences are distilled down to what the journalist considers the most essential elements. Part of this is excused because we are such a busy society that many of us just want a sound bite, not the whole story. It is not presented in its entirety for the reader to draw his or her own opinion. Typically, the result is superficial, even ruthlessly edited information that presents the opinion of the journalist as fact.

As a journalism teacher, my most difficult task was to help my budding journalists see the difference between fact and opinion. Even when facts are brought forward, the writer can skew the conclusion to be drawn by presenting only information that supports a specific point of view. Again, opinion, not news.

It is safe to say that in this age, officials are elected by the media. The fact that this pandemic struck in an election year is frustrating the public's ability to get solid news. Every politician vying for our votes in November is wooing the media and us along with them.

The pandemic has become a political game. When we should be getting straight information on the course of the virus – the absolutely necessary precautions – this political environment has hindered our access to accurate information.

Not all of us are worried about the veracity of the information we are receiving. There are those who choose to believe whatever they are told by government officials – most of whom are up for re-election. Never mind that every official seems to have his or her "pet" expert to back up their claims whether to keep us housebound or not, for example.

Because we are a sound-bite society, some of us are all too ready to take at face value whatever we are told. We want to get on with our lives. Just tell us what to do: mask, no mask, sequester, social distance, eat out, eat in, haircut, no haircut, go to church, or listen to a broadcast in our jammies.

The "zoom" setting on your computer sometimes brings very important elements into sight. We need to look deeper at what we are being told to find which information is accurate.

If we are to be a zoom society, let us zoom in, not out, scrutinizing those details.

*Granddaughters – Raina, Olivia and Hannah – joined me at an open table
in a fast food place on the rare occasion we could dine inside.
We were allowed to take off our masks while eating.*

Politics Run Amuck

I have never been much of a fan of politics, but I do
believe it used to be clearer who were the good guys and
the bad guys even 20 years ago.

I sometimes wonder why people aspire to public
office. I hope it's not just a desire for control. I fear,
however, that many do enter the political arena because
they want power to enact their own personal view of
life. We would expect, of course, that personal convictions, deeply held, should drive those who would take

office. What is concerning, however, is that some have convinced themselves that they truly "know best."

I was recently reminded that personal freedom is critically important. We are each so unique, with our own set of values gleaned from our own specific set of life circumstances and challenges. It is safe to say that many of us believe we have come upon some truths, as well we should. Wherein lies the danger, however, is whether "our" truth must be universally held.

A good friend recently advised me to use CBD oil – an extract from marijuana – for my chronic back pain. My friend knows that during my brief traipse in hippiedom I used marijuana. She also knows that I believe the drug not only suppressed my desire and ability to get anything done, but it truly was a gateway to other drugs.

I experienced – along with my husband – being "set free" from the power of this and other drugs when we both came to faith in Jesus, the Messiah. A fellow hippie-turned-believer prayed for us and we experienced "something" leave the room. My husband always said it was the spirit of marijuana. Whether it was that or "addiction," the result was that neither of us ever dabbled in drugs again.

I relate this story to tell how fervently I feel about never having anything to do with marijuana. As I told my friend, even if doctors assured me I would never be free of my pain unless I used CBD oil, I would decline. It's hard to convey how drugs take away personal freedom. If you have ever been there – or especially if you are there now – you know.

Personal freedom, that is being free to decide for myself what is good and true, is the basis of life itself. I know, of course, that my right to live as I see fit is tempered by allowing others to do the same. If people are helped by CBD oil, for example, I don't fault them. All I know is it is not for me personally. We all need the freedom to choose according to our own experiences. One is not right and the other wrong.

So, what's the connection to politics? I'm glad you asked! This year's pandemic, especially being in an election year, has brought out all the corona virus experts on all sides of the aisle. Pundits of every political ilk would make rules for everyone based on their own personal experiences. Some of them would only advise, but the more powerful make mandates. When a person has the political clout to speak us into house arrest, that's very serious.

Lest anyone get excited, I am not for persons getting the virus, but I am for there being much more personal freedom in how we interpret the conflicting authorities. I know that my age presents a vulnerability to this virus. I should be cautious and consider carefully any exposure I might get, or give. What I don't understand is why everyone has to stay home because I need to.

I can tell you that sometimes as a teacher I made the same mistake as I see politicians making now. A few times when I had a couple of kids acting up in class, I forbade everyone from an activity, not just the bad actors.

If you want to see some real angst, try that with a room of high school seniors. Fortunately, I had a good rapport with the class and we were able to discuss the situation. The end result was that the guilty students received consequences and the rest of the class did not.

It's as if government officials as a group fear that they need to eliminate our personal freedoms to choose to act appropriately because there are some who will choose to endanger others. What they fail to realize is that people hell-bent on breaking the rules are statistically going to figure out how to violate the standard or law anyway. A great example is gun control. There are those who would take away all guns because there are those who will use them illegally. The right to bear arms is protected by the Constitution.

I live in a state that has legislated our personal freedoms away in an effort to control some bad actors. They have the mistaken thought that if you control everyone with what you believe is a truth – or right – in every aspect of life, everyone will behave. They just ruled out life itself.

Freedom is not a political permission. It is a God-given right.

Rubinstein boys masked up and heading to a rare day at school: Micah, Lev, Eitan.

Under the Stethoscope

There are several people in my circle of family and friends who are medical professionals. Their take on CO-VID 19 is very much influenced by their access to up-to-the-minute medical reports, periodicals and announcements. They typically are not depending on what the media is presenting as "facts." As a group, they express concern that there is a growing cavalier attitude of the general public toward the various health precautions in place.

The rest of us are paying some attention to the continual press releases. In the ninth month of corona, varying – often contradictory – media reports flooded the airways. The various expert information from scientists going head to head. This one declares that the virus can live only a fleeting moment on surfaces, while another contends that the life cycle may be much more virulent. One medical authority provides studies to show that schools should be open, while another equally respected scientist contends that opening schools is tantamount to using the herd immunity philosophy of letting this virus "run its course."

Wherein lies the truth? How is the general public to determine the real facts of this pandemic? There has been a rising distrust of the medical community. Granted, this is a new virus so in the beginning everyone believed we should err on the side of caution, but at this stage we are facing economic, social and educational disaster worldwide. There is great social unrest that could probably be abated IF the public could be assured which medical professionals are accurate about the course of this virus.

When I listen to one of my best – and longtime friends – who is a nurse, I am assured that the situation is worse than we have been led to believe. Her conviction is "Caring is Wearing" in reference to whether we should all be masked. She recently told me that she felt we show our love for others by wearing a mask. She acknowledges that the wearer also has a level of protection from being hit with invisible droplets from even brief, casual conversations.

There is conflicting "scientific" evidence on the matter of masks. I tend to believe my friend. Even when I am outside of six feet from someone, a sudden sneeze or cough could expel up to 16 feet. That is a scientific fact I have known for many years.

I have found myself getting more lax about wearing

a mask in some settings. I think we probably all have an inner circle – or pod – of persons with whom we have been sequestering throughout this epidemic. With my family – which includes four households – I find myself going about business as usual without masking.

As my recent conversation with my friend made me realize, I have no way of knowing if my family members have had exposure in the course of their interactions with those outside our pod that they could be bringing back to us. In fact, a couple of my family members are in contact with the owners of sick animals on a daily basis. I do know they and their client's wear masks and endeavor to social distance.

In my son Josh's job as a teacher, he was conducting distance learning from his classroom until the school opened up a hybrid approach to school. My son is still masked on campus, alone in his classroom, and except for weekly teacher meetings, has little or no contact with others.

Josh's wife Rosemary works in a clinic where she wears a mask to consult with patients on the relation-ship of their diets to their health. Even though the clients are at this clinic for non-contagious illness, they each come from their families and whatever contact has been brought into their homes.

Several of the other adults in my circle pretty much work from home, including me. In that setting, we rarely encounter others, but we too go out for the occasional shopping or procurement of services. I don't even go into the post office to pick up mail in my box without wearing a mask and observing social distancing. At this time all places of business require masking for entrance.

There has to be a balance between fear and faith. I don't want to be worried about getting the virus to the point of acting irrationally and avoiding all contact with others. I don't want to err, however, on the other end of that spectrum, having faith that God is protecting me and will keep me from getting sick and getting lax about following the recommended preventative health protocols.

I am reminded we are not promised that we won't encounter troubles, even sickness. What we are promised is that God will see us through, even if it is "our time." I don't want to dare the enemy by being careless and expect God to get me out of it.

We dare not test our God. I've never known a dare that turned out well.

Baby Boomers make up a significant and vocal demographic in American society. Three of our family's sages: my sisters Carol and Elaine and I who are all quite opinionated. It is our age group that was the hardest hit. Praise God we survived!

Silencing the Sages

What would really bring people down? If you want to cripple a nation, a world, deny them access to their pool of wisdom. What a sinister idea!

When the pandemic was first declared, our government and health officials called for seniors to self isolate. Why? Because as with all flus, the elderly are the most vulnerable. The elderly and their attendant health conditions make this population more susceptible to not only catching viruses, but also lacking immune systems strong enough to fight them off.

From the outset of this disease, people over 65 have been the "target" group – my people. At first we were told to not congregate in groups larger than ten, while more virile Americans were still allowed to be among groups ten times larger. Then the call was made for total isolation of the old among us. Others are not even allowed to visit the elderly if they are in care facilities or hospitals unless they are at their "end of life," and even then the number of loved ones admitted is seriously restricted, usually to only one.

Even though the U.S. does not rank highest in having the most people 65 and older, its elders are some of the most influential in the world. The second largest demographic—almost 80 million—in the U.S. is the Baby Boomers. The Millennials do outnumber them, yet it is the Boomers who shape the American economy. It is not a stretch to say that as goes America, so goes the world. Boomers constitute the strongest lobby in the world.

Some would even go so far as to view this demographic as the greatest drain on our global resources. It's not the Millennials who are fighting to keep Social Security. Two-thirds of Baby Boomers think preserving Social Security and Medicare for themselves and future generations is even more important than reducing the deficit, according to a Pew Research survey.

Social media does allow for mingling in larger circles. The predominant voices, however, are not those of Boomers. In fact, the existence of our most-used cyber communication tools is due to Millennials. It is they who have massive control over access and what voices get heard.

And even if the creative genius for social media comes from the young here in Amereica, mass production of all hardware and software is centered in China.

The Chinese did not originate most of our disease-fighting medicines, yet they are the leaders in producing most of the medicines used around the world. China, from whence came the virus.

China has always had a population problem. They have used genocide on their own people to curtail their numbers especially by limiting children per family. As a nation, they do not rank high in persons over 65. They are not the world players they might be if their population boasted more of the elderly as do Japan, Italy and Portugal, to mention the top three homes to seniors. And then, of course, there is America and its Boomers.

I barely missed being a Boomer, but would be part of what was called the Silent Generation. And this is exactly what is expected of me. Six million died when voices were silent. This pandemic is masking a horrifying holocaust. There are over 600 million people 65 and older in the world.

How could such a virulent virus get loose on the world? The world powers scurry about pushing for control of weapons of mass destruction. How did this one slip through? And how could it get away with targeting our most productive and creative people group? The battle is not in the silo but the test tube. Let's put more of our creative energies into isolating the vaccine and less on controlling the movements of the very ones who might think us out of this tank.

Bring the best medical practices to the aid of our senior sages so their voices will not be silenced. Without their wisdom we don't stand a chance against this and similar global threats.

Respecting our elders is not an idle adage.

Most of the family made it to the cemetery for the 10th anniversary of my husband Rube's death in November of 2020. LtoR Grandkids. Front: Olivia, Micah, Hannah, Ava, Raina. Middle: Eitan, Lev, Eliana. Back: Sarah Annemarie, Corey, Sarai. All accounted for except Ryan who couldn't make it that day.

The Cull

Your eyes are not failing you. I am talking about a cull, not a call.

When the coronavirus first became public knowledge, the immediate thought that came to mind was that this pandemic was a cull – a cutting away of the elderly and infirm.

I know the thought did not come from me. Was it God? Perhaps, but I know the reality of this being a cull of primarily the elderly was very personal. I'm right in the middle of the target demographic due to being in my 70's and having a couple of health conditions.

Nature has a way of sweeping through living things and getting rid of the weak. We see it in herds of deer and other animals in the wild. In a sense, it is the acting out of the survival of the fittest, which is supposed to strengthen herds. I suppose that can apply to people as well.

The elderly of any species are less able to provide their own sustenance and care. In America we provide care facilities to accommodate as we decline physically and mentally. There is Social Security for those 65 and older but that fund has atrophied, barely providing the basics to its recipients.

The magnitude of money being expended to maintain the lives and quality of life of our older citizens, has raised red flags for economists. Our seniors, however, have the ability to share with others how to better navigate life.

Sometimes just by virtue of the wealth of experiences we have had and the troubles we have survived, we are left with wisdom to impart. It can be argued that we have an important place in the general scheme of things. There is the potential for subsequent peoples to make fewer or at least different mistakes as they heed our advice.

So, I ask myself, why would a world pandemic – or plague – be important at this time in man's history? I believe this question requires our attention. Have we done anything that has contributed to this toxic situation?

We are in a world climate where life is not universally considered precious. In fact, China itself has been one of the biggest devaluers of life. Their attitude affects their policy for taking care of their people. Or not.

Our current outbreak of the coronavirus came from a lab in China. China does not know how to provide its citizens with food and other basic needs. If this virus did come from a bat or other contaminated critter, it's assumed these people were scrounging at the bottom of the food chain – eating rodents – to sustain their life.

In order for China to guarantee that families have no more than one child, abortions are not only legal but pushed on the people. In terms of providing for abortions, China is second only to New York. This is the ultimate disregard for life, and the most heinous offense is making policy based on an unborn child being a fetus, not a child yet, thus disposable as so much tissue.

Regardless of all the reasons this is fatally shortsighted, it is grievous for us to kill our children regardless of our belief system. At the most vulnerable and dependent time of human life – in utero – a life can be legally terminated. We're good at euphemisms, too. We say "terminated" or even "end a pregnancy" to avoid describing the horrors that the unborn child experiences as he or she is aborted.

Never in the history of the world have so many people been murdered. Statistics indicate that America alone has killed 62 million babies since the courts made it a Constitutional right in 1973 with Roe vs. Wade. Over 1.6 billion have been killed worldwide since 1980. I will note that the site offering these statistics indicated they were mostly reporting on "surgical abortions." Another site, the Pharmacists for Life Organization, estimates that there have been about 250 million babies aborted chemically since 1973. (www.pfli.org)

So, how is this connected to our elderly? Good question. It devastates me to say that it is my generation who has authorized this killing field. In 1973 I was about 30 years old. My generation, mostly Baby Boomers, are estimated to presently (2020) be numbered at about 73 million. What an impact we have had! Of course, there have been some great contributions. All would concede that it is our demographic that has been the most influential in the history of the world in the last 50 years. All big decisions in that time period were made by us. Even Roe vs. Wade.

It is my generation that has found cures for diseases and even found out how to prolong life. We are living longer but what legacy are we leaving? The irony is that we were simultaneously dismantling life. We've seen horrific genocide worldwide. My generation is first on the bandwagon to seek equal rights, fair treatment and global responsibility. How is it that we can miss the glaring loss of life at our own hands?

The cull. There is a Scale of Justice. How can any good we have done ever outweigh the innocent lives we have taken. It can't and doesn't.

Those of us who survive must work to take apart the killing machine lest we become the targets of the next cull.

To quote bestselling author Michael Connelly's famous detective, Harry Bosch, "Everybody counts or nobody counts."

-F-
FUTURE & FORECAST

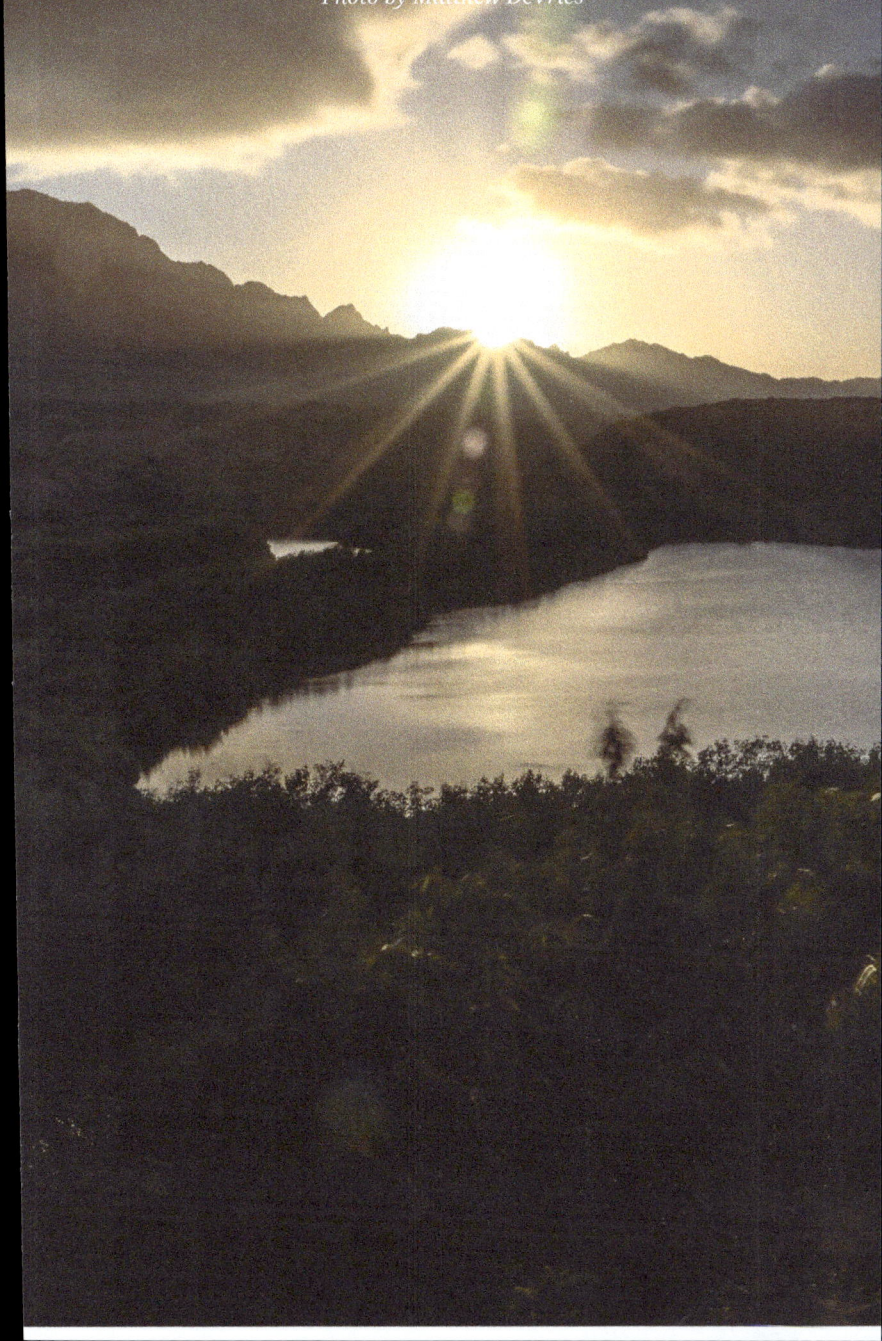

Hopeful for the future even in dark times.
After the storm the sun breaks through.

Photo by Matthew DeVries

Seven of my grandchildren who are definitely of this new generation.
Front: Raina and Eliana - BFF's; Center: Lev.
Top LtoR: Olivia, Micah, Hannah and Eitan.

Generation "V"

V is for virtual. What will history say about this generation of young people now? I am afraid if we look at what all they have been through, we might even call them distant.

We thought we had troubles enough with the entitlement issues of the Millennials. According to Pew Research, anyone born between 1981 and 1996 (ages 24 to 39 in 2020) is considered a Millennial. Some round these dates to be persons born from 1980 to 2000. Contrast their in-your-face demands with the kids coming up.

Those born from roughly 1997 until about 2015 are Generation Z. They received their first mobile phone at about age 10. Many of them had early technology exposure playing on their parents' phones or tablets. They have grown up in a hyper-connected, albeit virtual, world. According to kasasa.com– a financial and technology service company – the smart phone is this generation's preferred method of communication, on which they spend an average of three hours a day. That does not include how much time they are on other devices.

This much use of technology has been known to mesmerize children. They get very involved with the programs they access electronically. I have watched kids this age appear to be in a hypnotic state while playing these games.

Today's children were already being criticized for having too much "screen" time. When they are not otherwise engaged, they could be found playing video games or involved in other online activities. I know more than one family that limits their kids' screen time.

And now all of those kids are in front of that same screen, this time experiencing mandated distance learning. A common complaint of the kids is that parents won't let them have as much personal use of technology because they have already been hooked up for so many hours daily just doing their schoolwork.

What we know about screen time is not just about the quality of the content. Parents do raise legitimate concerns about exposure to violent apps. Kids are also becoming very dependent on a virtual world where there is no real personal connection. That is who this new generation is. They could be "Z" for zoned out.

In contrast to the Millennials, this generation might

never get in your face at all. They tend to be detached from human interaction. They endure their actual face time with people until they can be released back to their screens.

I have studied just enough of psychology to know that when human beings cut themselves off from others, this detachment is a disorder. What can we expect from kids coming up in this virtual environment? It is a concern.

And this pandemic has just made it worse. How do we get the kids off their computers when they are required to sit at them up to seven hours a day just to get their education?

First, I hope we can influence the powers that be to "Let our children go." It sounds like an anti-slavery slogan, and it is! The longer the schools are kept closed, the more distant our kids become. Some might mistakenly think that kids are getting more personally connected with their education because the teacher can see everyone's little postage-size face. Don't be misled.

As I sit with my grandkids doing distance learning, I watch them disconnect. These kids are coming up with a new set of ways to disengage while class is going on. The younger the child, the harder it is for him or her to even sit that long. The kindergarten program has the kids get up for wiggle breaks, but there is no such respite for the older kids.

Second, we must try to re-engage our kids. How will a detached generation take over our world? It is bigger than just breaking off the chains of the pandemic. We need to actively encourage our young ones to get up and move. They need to get out of the house. They need to be playing sports again, or for the first time. They need to have a hobby or other activity that takes them beyond the screen. We need to give them opportunities to use their imaginations.

Third, we need to have a game plan if – when? – such a worldwide crisis happens again. To me one of the biggest losses of this pandemic and its restrictions has been the loss of spontaneity in our children. The confinement has been deadening.

A popular Bible proverb (Proverbs 29:18) asserts, "Where there is no vision, the people perish." Our vision for the future is realized in our children. What we need to take from that is, without our children, we perish. They are the future and it is being determined right now for all of us.

Some may call this Generation Z. If they are instead Generation V, let it be for Victorious, not Virtual.

Familes stocked up on food and other scarce items during the pandemic. Life-long friends: Emily Glacken, my granddaughters Raina Whitley and Eliana Rubinstein.

Doomsday Preppers Delight

What will you do with five-gallon buckets of soybeans 40 years later? Don't laugh. I think there are those among us who are not aware that the Hippie Age in this country was a lot about preparing for the impending Apocalypse.

When my husband and I retreated to a remote plot of land in the mountains of northern New Mexico – actually on the Continental Divide – we were driven there by fears of Doomsday. At that time we were not guided by a spiritual connection with God, but I am sure we were being influenced by spirits of the other realm. God is not the purveyor of such fear.

We had a meager income at the time, having both withdrawn from society as a whole to go off grid. I had about $4000 from cashing in my teacher retirement fund after only six years of teaching. It was 1973, so that amount had great buying power. It was enough to "grub-stake" us to "homestead." I don't use these terms lightly.

We did indeed need to lay in tools and provisions to sustain us in the isolated place we intended to be the scene of our survival while the world was undergoing severe trials. Our destination was a ten-acre piece of property owned by the parents of one of our fellow hippies. Technically we weren't homesteading, but we romanticized that we were.

One of our first tasks – after readying the soil for planting our food – was to drive to the nearest town to get supplies. We had goats and chickens on the property and planned to grow enough vegetables to eat and preserve for winter. We set out to purchase grains and beans. Somewhere along the line we had acquired clean five-gallon buckets for long-term storage of dry foods. Hence, the buckets of soybeans. Our stash also included rice, wheat, pinto beans and oats.

I don't remember at what point we decided to get rid of our stored food, but it was some years after we returned to society. Having become believers in God, we no longer saw hoarded food as a solution for worldwide chaos, but we came out of the mountains still needing our stored provisions. We ground our own flour from the wheat and cracked and toasted some of the grain for hot cereal. At some point, however, soybeans go rancid. Fortunately, by then we both had jobs and the means to purchase fresh foods.

The Preppers of today feel very vindicated for their choice to be prepared to go off grid. When they see the chaos, the empty shelves and even the looting we have experienced this year, I am sure they are patting themselves on the back for having already stocked their storehouses.

A documentary on some of these folks showed them as typically ultra military with all kinds of weaponry. I watched as they put a couple through some intense testing of their survival skills and preparedness in order to determine if they would be trusted to become part of this cell group. I don't remember if the man and wife passed the tests, but what hit me was that this kind of mentality is all about survival being a solitary solution to a global threat.

They obviously do not trust humans to help one another during these times. Instead, they seem to believe that when the times get tough, people will turn on one another. They believe they will only survive if they take matters into their own hands, not relying on any but a select few.

Do I believe that there are some depraved souls who would "take me out" in a heartbeat? Yes. I am not naïve. But I believe we are part of a much larger picture from the Creator of the universe and all living things. He put a bit of His Spirit in each of us. We have that spark that loves all living things. We have that unselfish, giving sense that would cause us to share our last crumb of bread with another.

When all is said and done, someday there will be an Apocalypse. If we can believe the Bible – which I obviously do – when that time comes there will be some who turn against their fellow man, but to what avail? I believe our God has already prepared a plan for each of us to get us through the future storms. Might we die? Sure.

But, He has promised us that we don't have to do massive undertakings to prepare but to primarily put our individual trust in Him and our fellow human beings.

If we end up with a full cupboard, we share. We lay down our lives for each other as God himself did for us by sacrificing his Son, Jesus. We see the bigger picture when adversity strikes.

So, you might want to rethink your buckets of food. Being prepared in itself is not bad, but relying on your own ability to stave off calamity is foolish.

You could do all that prepping and die from eating stored food gone rancid.

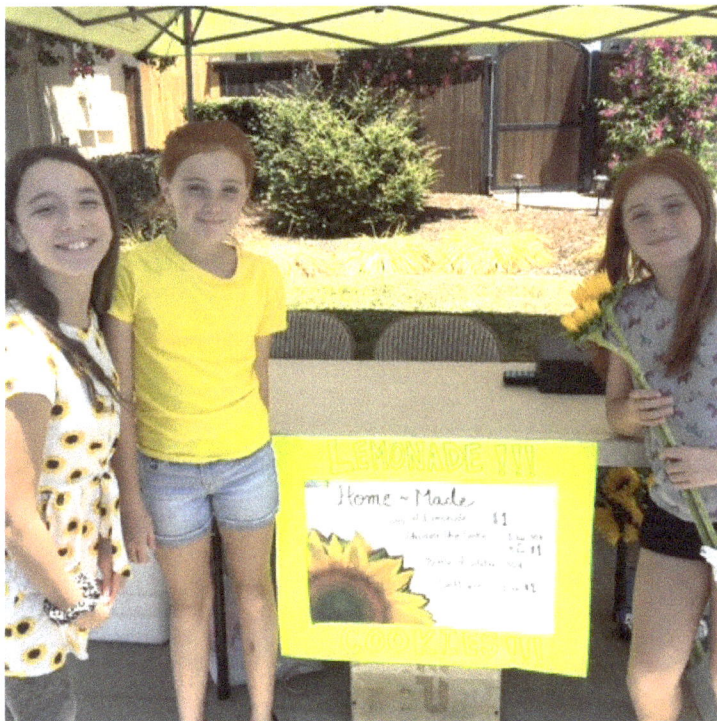

Lemonade stand of Whitley girls Olivia and Hannah, with their friend far left: Ariana. Lemons to lemonade.

Turning Bad to Good

I wrote this piece three years ago, but chose to use it in this collection of writings for what I believe will become obvious.

Today I was not my better self. I found myself in a situation where I felt my rights had been violated. What did I do? I exploded on the perceived perpetrator.

The scene was haggling over who was there first for a parking space. Sound familiar? I hope you did better than I did. When the guy drove in front of me into the space for which I had been waiting, I honked. No response. I honked again. Nothing. I sat on my horn.

At that point a little family was getting out of their car across from the contested parking spot. They began to yell at the man who had taken the spot, defending my claim. He yelled back. As he then walked past my vehicle, I declared out my window that I had been waiting before he got there. He said he was there first and proceeded with a threat, "I have your license number!"

My yucky self said, "Someday this will happen to you." He kept walking into the medical building. I kept circling for a spot. After parking, I actually encountered the man who had already conducted his business—it looked like he was just dropping something off—and was returning to his car.

I stopped him with the calm and genuinely curious question, "What made you think what you did was right?" He responded that he was there first and saw when I drove up. He continued by complaining how that man and wife kept verbally haranguing him all the way into the clinic.

At that moment, I knew what I had to do. I sincerely said to him that I honestly had not seen his car when I arrived, as he had approached from around a corner. I wondered to myself if he had seen me drive up the second time as I had backed up to give the previous car in the spot more room to navigate their exit. Never mind. No longer relevant.

I immediately apologized for my behavior and for setting him up to be assaulted by well-meaning strangers. I even asked him to please forgive me, and that I was truly sorry. He looked at me with a blank expression on his face. We each went our opposite way.

As I went about my business at the clinic, I couldn't get that young family out of my mind. I really wanted them to see that I was the one who probably did not see the situation correctly and definitely acted out of control.

I was at the appointment for a full hour. As I was exiting the building, I was aware of a man mentioning something about "that lady" to a woman, apparently his wife. I had a fleeting thought it might have been the same couple, but couldn't believe they could actually still be there. I did not know what they looked like, only that they were young.

As I proceeded out the doors, the man—carrying a two-year-old boy—caught up with me asking if I was the lady in the parking spot dispute. What?! Amazing they were still around.

I told him about the talk I had with the alleged parking spot thief and how I ended up apologizing. My avenging angel—who I then learned was Jeff—was adamant that they saw the whole thing and that I had definitely been there first.

I truly believe God gave me this opportunity to speak life into a situation that I had allowed to escalate. Regardless of who was there first, I had a choice in my reaction. I could have accepted that for some reason the man truly believed he was first to the spot—he had stated that he had circled three times up to then—and I could have given him the benefit of the doubt.

Who should yield in such a case? "The one who is more spiritually mature." Well, it wasn't me at that moment, BUT it should have been.

I could have been grateful for all God has forgiven me, all the undeserved blessings I have received. How could I be stingy with blessings and not allow one to this total stranger who definitely felt he was being wrongly accused.

As it happens, the Lord allowed for blessing out of my willingness to turn—*teshuva*—from my selfish ways. I gave Jeff my card, which stated I was a writer/publisher. He was excited to let me know that his wife is a writer looking for a way to publish. A sweet connection.

God is good. He knows we are not perfect, but in His amazing grace, He not only forgave me, but gave me an opportunity to set things right. He knows our frame (Psalm 103:14), how we are tempted, how and when we are vulnerable to exhibiting our "old" unredeemed selves, and, in my case, my indignant self-righteous self.

I do pray the man I accosted got a taste of God's love for Him. I know the Lord will not allow him to have a setback in his relationship with His creator out of this. Quite the contrary, out of what we—and even Satan—intends for evil, God will turn to good (Genesis 50:20) if we are willing to humble ourselves (James 4:10).

How then shall we live during this pandemic?

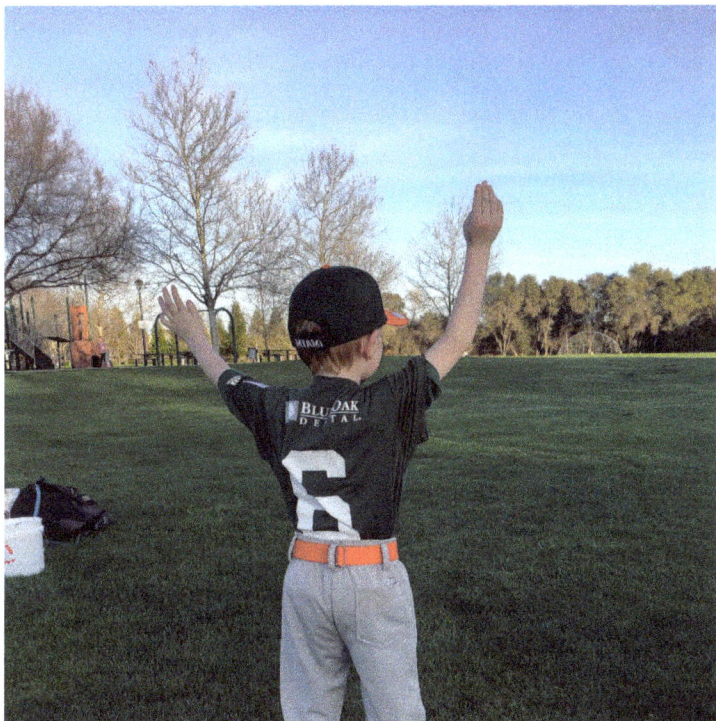

A rare view of an opening in the sky.

Breaking Free

I am reminded of a recurring dream I used to have. In it, the earth is full of turmoil. Everyone is running to and fro. There is a sense that the Apocalypse is coming. I remember feeling the need to find my loved ones and get them on a spaceship that was poised to leave the earth, pointed skyward. I knew there was not enough room for everyone to get on board so I was frantically trying to gather up my family.

At that moment, the sky opened up as if a giant can

opener was peeling back the sky. The ship was posi-
tioned to fly through this new opening. It was at that
moment that we all realized the world we were leaving
was not reality.

It seems so apropos when I look at what our world is
going through during this pandemic. Some people are
calling it the New Normal. Everything in our lives has
shifted. After almost a year of living under the COVID
19 threat, we are not only used to the new ways, but
we are creatively buying in. We have new businesses
popping up providing us the services needed to live this
changed life. Not the least of which is the sign businesses
who have made all the signage for social distancing and
masking.

Mask makers are in their element – so many designs
from which to choose. It's a whole new fashion statement. Masks convey not just people's favorite things,
but their attitude toward the mask wearing itself. I have
seen ones that show huge smiles. Many reflect fields of
employment of the wearers.

An interesting aspect to seeing only half of people's
faces is that we are left to read eyes to match up with
their muffled words. We have become used to seeing
only people's eyes. All of the facial cues we would normally rely on to give fuller meaning to what someone is
saying are no longer available to us. Smirks or smiles go
completely unnoticed. My friend who is almost totally
deaf is very frustrated that she is not able to read lips
without asking someone to remove the mask.

It has been said that the eye is the window to the soul.
If that is true, perhaps we are now seeing into people's
souls, and they into ours. Perhaps. If previously we had
been using the rest of our facial features to express
ourselves, we no longer have that option. Sometimes we
might have used our full expression to distract from –

and conceal? – what our truthful eyes might be saying. We might be revealing much more than we intended from the cover of our mandated masks.

Another industry that has taken a huge boost is Amazon. Prior to this pandemic, I ordered a few things online from Amazon and some from a provider of other goods. For the last year I have found myself looking on-line for every purchase but food. And speaking of food, the grocery stores have risen to the New Normal by providing the most detailed online purchasing of their products, which they also deliver to your door.

What's missing from this upsurge in businesses is those that would promote any kind of socializing, bonding. There's no organized sports – even at the Little League or Pop Warner level – plus no concerts or other performances. The government has decided these are not essential.

All organizations and businesses have had to recreate themselves, but the result is that there is almost no personal interaction between folks. The downside is that we learn from each other when we have the chance to discuss things, which is not happening these days. When we collaborate, we discover things. We might even discover that this New Normal is a façade.

If this existence is indeed a gear up for the real world to come, our greatest mistake will be allowing ourselves to be disconnected as families, as society. When the chaos of my dream – nightmare? – loomed, it was people I sought to take with me to freedom, not things. Perhaps I was having difficulty rounding up my kin because we had lost connection.

If we want to know what the real world is, we must look up. Looking around us will give us false impressions of where life is going. Scripturally, we know that our salvation comes from God. He is the way out of this dilemma.

Any one of us could be the conduit by which all our loved ones are saved. Look up, our redemption draws nigh.

Our family didn't let COVID or the fires keep us from celebrating or getting our "pod" together. LtoR Front: Raina, Micah, Hannah, Olivia, "Penny" the dog, Lev. Middle: Uncle Jacob, Sarah Annemarie, Uncle Michael and Aunt Sarah, Corey, Sarai, Uncle Joshua holding Ava with Eitan behind, Aunt Rosemary, Eliana and me. Back: Ryan and Aunt Monicqua.

Color Me Content

Be content no matter the situation in which you find yourself. I have believed in these words from the Bible most of my life. I know we are to be satisfied – at peace – in whatever circumstances we find ourselves. For me, this has been an intellectual assent all these years, but my heart has gone another direction.

Do you sometimes find yourself questioning – perhaps even God Himself – why and how you could be in the position, situation, condition in which you find yourself? Do you find yourself yearning for when that will change? Do you envision what life could/should/would be that better suits your aspirations? Join the human club.

Today marks a turning point for me. I know the rhetoric. God is totally aware of the bad circumstances around us. His promises always seem to be about how He will never leave us nor forsake us. He will be there with us in the middle of the storm.

Biblically, it is rare for the sufferer to be totally plucked out of the circumstance. Quite the contrary. The situation swirls around and around, but our Lord is in the midst of it with us, be it a dangerous relationship, a terrifying fire, a world pandemic, even a lion's den (Psalm 23:4). That's the promise. God is not a man – or mankind – that He could lie.

Sometimes even in the smallest of dangers, we realize how we have been spared by a loving God. There is no aspect of our lives too big or small for the Lord. Sometimes it is difficult for us to be at peace no matter what things are thrown our way. If we can believe that God not only knows our troubles, but has provided a way for us to overcome them in every situation, perhaps we can be content in our circumstances (Romans 15:13).

Sometimes we question why we are who we are. Why were we born into whatever families we have, why are we part of various cultures, why do we have our features and not those of someone we admire? A recent conversation with a friend was very revealing. She was discouraged that she was not born into a different ethnic group. It's not that she is part of an oppressed ethnicity – quite the contrary – but she felt that there was one people group that God might love more. It troubled her to the point of thinking of converting, which is something that is acceptable in her desired identity.

It was when I was assuring her that God could have just as easily had her born into her desired culture that I realized how true that is. My late husband used to say that God made all the ethnicities on purpose. There are no second-class citizens in God's world plan. Therefore, God made both my friend and me just as He planned.

What a relief. I don't have to worry that I am not where God can find me. These are trying times, but I know that I am in God's hands. I can relax and not be afraid. I believe God and that is what faith is. God will fulfill His purposes in me. Nothing this world can throw at me – or you – can change His plans. He not only knew all we would encounter, but He planned whatever counter-measures were needed to keep us in His arms. Wherever He is, there is peace and joy.

Winds may blow, ashes rain down, viruses threaten, but nothing can keep us from the peace of God. He will continue His work in us. As hard as it might be to believe, we are exactly where God knew we would be. He will quiet the storms, but in the meantime He wants us to trust Him, "Be still and know that [He] is God" (Psalm 46:10).

I am reminded of the book, Color Me Beautiful. The premise is that we are beautiful no matter what. The suggestion is that we can enhance our features by wearing shades of colors that complement who God made us to be.

Applying this to the spiritual, we are wonderfully made in the image of our Lord. We can be the best "version" of ourselves when we put on the full armor of God (Ephesians 6:10-18). The way God protects the heart, mind and soul is complete. It is this covering that causes us to stand against whatever the enemy throws at us. We are wearing God's righteousness and equipped with His promises from his Word. We can relax under God's protection.

I am content. And you?

The long day ends for a new day to begin.
Hopeful. "Red sky at night, sailor's delight."
There will be wind in our sails.

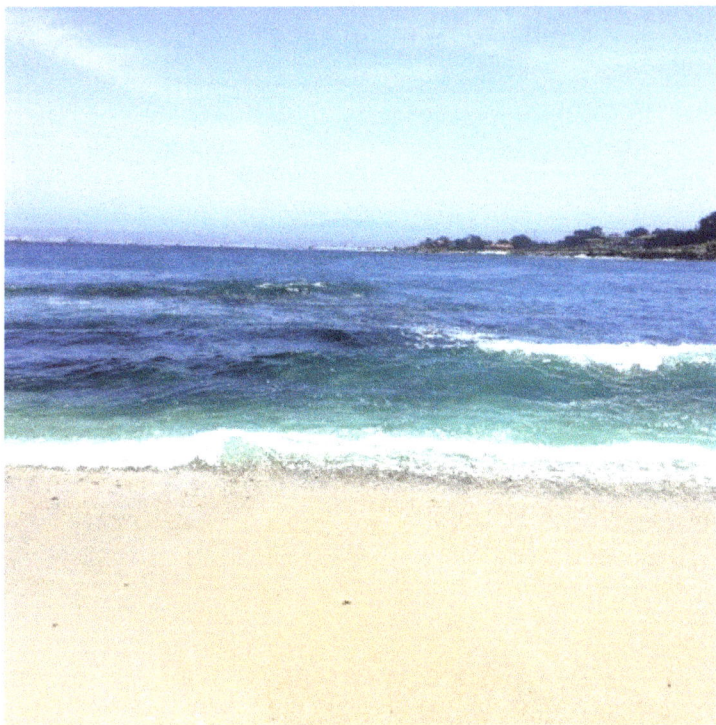

Before COVID hit, our extended family got to vacation in Kauai. This image reflects how bright and beautiful our days were. It was truly the calm before the storm.

Bright Sunshiny Day

The major part of this storm has passed. The sun is coming out. The dark clouds are leaving. As things clear up, we are left to put into perspective what happened.

The 2020 elections are just behind us. Politicians on both sides of the aisle have used COVID 19 as a vote getter, so the expectation had been that after all ballots were in, depending upon who got in office, things would settle down. Or not. The jury is still out on that.

The initial counting of the ballots supported Biden having been elected, but President Trump believed there had been discrepancies in the ballot counting. The Electoral College has met and declared Biden our new president. Even with the election settled, it is still difficult to know if we are getting accurate information about the impact of COVID.

What an amazing feeling, however, to be on the "other side" of the peak of the pandemic. We have had mostly a gradual move to ending the shutdowns. There were stages, primarily dependent on numbers of occurrences of new cases of the virus in a given county or city, ostensibly because there was a fear that our medical facilities could not keep up with the demand. Another variable has been how "essential" the service was deemed for when it could be reopened.

What did we learn? We did realize how resourceful and creative we could be about how to continue at least a minimum of services. We also learned that what the government considers essential is often not lined up with what many Americans value. Faith-based organizations were relegated to the lowest rating of importance to continue. That says a lot about this country's politicians as a whole.

What we didn't learn is that when there is a target group that is more vulnerable to the threat – any threat – the decision to shut everyone down is an overreaction. We knew our elderly and health-compromised population could die from this virus. What did we do? We "warehoused" the elderly and infirm into assisted living institutions. We didn't allow their families to visit and help take care of them. Many died, and did so alone.

We kept everyone from playing in parks, going to school and work, getting haircuts, attending big venue events – even their own graduation ceremonies – when we could have just warned the vulnerable to stay home so they weren't at risk, but giving them that choice. Why did that have to be so politically charged?

Even if everyone had worn masks to keep up our usual routines, especially given what we know now, that would have been enough. Some officials were aware very early on, even before the pandemic was declared, that some of the mandated precautions were probably overly cautious. If the speaking voice travels up to six feet and the virus does not live on surfaces but a moment, then why did we shut everything and everyone down?

There is evidence key medical officials knew this fact very early on. Politicians were very guarded about which stance they endorsed, always with an eye to their continued "service" to the people. The political machine was allowed to impact proposed best-pandemic-practices.

There are citizens who applaud the government's response to the pandemic. I am not one of them. This is not just hindsight speaking. Political figures took advantage of the chaos to take complete control of our society. Fear ran amuck. How could we go along with such severe restrictions without more scientific proof of the necessity? But, the better question is, how can the government take away our choice that violates both our Constitutional and God-given rights? How could it ever be okay to deprive us of our fundamental hard-fought freedoms?

Many places of business suffered greatly, some even shutting their doors permanently. Cafés and restaurants had their revenue decreased significantly, and some closed to never reopen again. Services such as beauty and barber shops were hard hit because they could not social distance while still performing their services. Even medical and dental offices could not provide more than emergency care. All restrictions mandated by elected officials.

Can we guarantee that people put into office to serve us will not again do us such a disservice? There were several recalls in the works, one against our own governor. It is increasingly more difficult to really know candidates prior to their getting elected. Once persons are in office, it is almost impossible to effectively stop them from violating our constitutional guarantees. The old adage has never been more true – "Absolute power corrupts absolutely."

So we have come full circle. We are back to the way these writings began. We first looked at Huxley's Brave New World. It is eerie, and has been devastating, the similarities of our society during this pandemic to that dystopian society. Relationships were not valued, even criminally discouraged, babies' fate can be determined by the state, and those in power got to decide what were essential services and even essential persons and set up policies and procedures to enforce such.

Sound a little too familiar? We still refer to Huxley's "science fiction" work as representing a dystopian society, where, by definition, persons lead "wretched, dehumanized, fearful lives" that are not to be desired. (Merriam-Webster Dictionary) I am in good company as I take a closer look at the state of our governing bodies in relation to our personal freedoms being violated.

Brave New World? It's a new world, but certainly not brave by anyone's standards. Yes, there have been many brave people, not the least of which have been the healthcare professionals, but on the whole we are left with a world that looks very different, but not in a good way.

The sun is out at this moment. We see a rainbow that Biblically was the way God showed people the storm was over. This occurred first after the Great Flood where God cleansed the earth of all its defiant acts by reducing the population to one family, Noah's. The heavenly sign of the rainbow was also to assure us that He would never use a flood again to get our attention.

Our Creator didn't say, however, that there would never be another global disaster. This is where we can exercise our God-given freedom of choice. Let's think twice before putting people in office. Let's be sure they share the majority values of our society. We must choose persons to represent us who put a high value on the rights of us all.

We have to have people running the show who care more about the people than their own popularity and prosperity.

Reaching up. "Our redemption draws nigh."
Photo by Jonas Ferlin

The Call

The big question is, "Was God trying to get our attention?" As with any devastating situation, God assures us that He will use it to get us to change if something is amiss. If so, we all need to first look deep within ourselves and then look globally. What have we allowed to occur that grieves our Creator?

I am not alone in noting that the answer is in who God is. He himself created all forms of life. He himself set aside some things as being sacred, sanctified, life being first and foremost. Have we violated the sanctity of life? Millions of aborted babies cry out to the Creator. Have we violated the sanctity of marriage? How can we promote homosexuality as normal when God Himself told us He created gender to assure life goes on.

Both of these violations have brought down many civilizations, not the least of which was Israel. The sanctity of life including distinction for mutual blessing is who God is.

Court-sanctioned abortion and the normalizing of homosexuality have been man's attempt to solve two perceived problems in our world.

Abortion is a horrific solution – a "Final Solution"? – to the number of souls on the earth. We shudder when we watch global genocides. How can we use euphemisms, just semantics to exclude the killing of babies from our horror?

Likewise, our hearts break for children who are not validated as being made in the image of the Creator. We yearn for them to know that they are not a mistake. God would not tell us that He created us as who we are – especially our gender – and then tell us, "Oops, some of you got trapped in the wrong bodies." We even give them the sacred sign of the rainbow to give them the illusion of now being beautiful in their chosen identity.

Yes, we are to offer hope for the safety of children from the time they are in the uterus through their development. That process is about affirming, not diverting them from God's purposes.

So, is God trying to get our attention? How could He let these man-made solutions continue? I don't know how God would meet the needs of a potentially overpopulated world and lovingly heal children to be glad in how they were made, BUT I do know He has a solution.

We are impatient people. Any time we find ourselves re-creating what the Creator put in place, it should give us serious pause.

We can't talk out of both sides of our mouth, so to speak. On one hand we own the God-given principle of "Loving our neighbor as ourselves," regardless of our religious affiliation. We care about people's rights. Americans agree that everyone has the right to "the pursuit of happiness" that our founders guaranteed us.

We can't take one of God's principles without acknowledging the others. Every life is valuable to our God. He has called each of us into this life. He knew our names BEFORE He formed us in the womb (Jeremiah 1:5). He made the critical decision of whether we would be boys or girls and equipped us accordingly – "male and female He created them." (Genesis 5:2)

To violate these two principles is to devalue the One who created us. God can't ignore the pain of His people forever. What He will do, however, is to give us a chance to correct our behavior and to turn from that way of living.

There are many who believe this pandemic is God's call to His people to turn from evil. He will forgive. Further, as we "humble ourselves and pray, and seek His face, turn from our evil ways, then we will hear from heaven, and He will FORGIVE our sin and heal our LAND." (2 Chronicles 7:14)

He is not unloving and is still ready to forgive. Individually and corporately we must search our souls and turn from our wicked ways. His promises even include the healing of our land if we do. He yearns to deliver us rather than sit in judgment.

It's all well and good to find the antivirus, but the real cure is at a deeper level. God is calling us to a deeper healing. It is for us to answer.

"Yes, God…"

AND NOW ... ?

Two roads...

The Aftermath

And they only recently stopped counting the presidential election ballots in January of this new year 2021. By mid November 2020, the media had "called" the election in favor of Biden. That's to be expected because our media – with few exceptions – have expended all their resources to promote the Democratic ticket.

It reminds me of when we were kids and we "called" that something was ours. "I call shotgun!" "I call first at bat!" There is no power nor authority in that declaration. I guess you will allow someone to call something if it benefits you as well.

President Trump's search for irregularities, discrepancies, even embedded algorithms that could have disrupted or skewed the voting process have not turned up legal proof within the time limit. All the states have certified their elections and the Electoral College was just convened to confirm Joe Biden is our President-elect.

Were there anomalies that could have skewed the election? What we do know is that our electoral system has some serious flaws. First and foremost is that not all states have the same requirements for someone to be able to obtain a ballot, i.e. register to vote. In my state of California, it is not required to show a photo ID to register to vote nor to cast a vote at the polling station.

Second, we know that this year officials sent out ballots to any person believed to be a registered voter ostensibly to help them vote during this pandemic. There are numerous reports of duplication of ballots, for example, an Olympic wrestling hopeful who had not resided in Arizona for over a year and had already voted in his new state was notified of his ballot "being accepted" in Arizona. Supposedly it had been turned in for counting, signature-verified, when he had never touched it.

There were likewise testimonies of innumerable cases of deceased persons being sent ballots that someone used to cast a vote. With there being no necessity for voters to personally bring in their ballots and being marked off as having voted, the accountability was shot.

Such irregularities could be anomalies, or not. Then we heard of whole batches of ballots received too late for the vote being allowed to be added to the totals. Recounts, verifications resulted.

As the election results were hanging in the air, we mere citizens were left to continue to make sense of our lives. Coronavirus is evidently not through as new spikes are popping up. Schools in our county were sufficiently in the "color" zone indicating "acceptable" cases of the virus and were allowed to open right after the November election. Those schools in California that were planning to reopen weeks later were told to delay until further notice if their counties reflected too many new cases of COVID.

At the beginning of our rainy season, and on the day of our first rain, state officials announced that restaurants in many counties in California can no longer serve indoors due to spikes. Evidently the restaurant lobby in some counties was strong enough to fight off the new closure citing the bad weather would pretty much shut them down permanently. With a new spike in cases, at this writing all restaurants can only serve takeout. The battle continues.

And they say there is now a vaccine – actually three different vaccines – for the coronavirus. Reportedly the vaccines are 95% effective at either keeping those vaccinated from getting the virus or lessening the severity of the virus if contracted. And, of course, there is the inevitable question of whether this virus can mutate such that it will no longer be affected by the vaccines just developed. Although a vaccine was not expected to be available until late in 2021, they were pushed through all the trials and released to the first wave of recipients – healthcare professionals – just last week.

An aftermath, by definition, reflects conditions once a bad situation has lifted. We really can't logically call the state we are in the aftermath. I am beginning to wonder if we will ever think of this pandemic and all its ramifications as being over.

One thing that has happened which could lead us to believe we will never return to any semblance of what used to be normal is that we have become used to officials taking over every aspect of our lives. There are some of us who used to rail against "big government." Now we have become accustomed – conditioned? – to do as we are told even as our civil liberties are systematically removed.

It is within us to keep finding order in whatever is thrown our way. We adapt. That is human nature.

What might they tell us next...

ABOUT THE AUTHOR

Shari Rubinstein is a wordsmith. She is an avid reader with her studies focused on a variety of life's teachings.

Her educational preparation includes a BA and MA in English, an MA in Special Education and a Madrikah license for teaching Messianic Judaism.

Shari is a retired English and journalism teacher. She has written for most of her life. Shari has most recently published her memoir: Becoming Ruth: dropout to teacher, hippie to straight, spiritualist to believer.

This current publication is the third compilation of her perspective pieces, which was preceded by Shift: Tiny Tales to Lighten Your Load and Phoenix: Rising Anew, Transformed by Fire.

The author lives in the greater Sacramento, California, area surrounded by her children and grandchildren and a loving community of extended family, friends, colleagues and fellow Believers.

To enjoy more of Shari Rubinstein's writing please visit:

www.ShariRubinstein.com

On her website you can enjoy her regular blog posts (which often become her books!) ... and you can order any of her books for yourself or others.

If you enjoyed this book, you will love Shari's other works: "Shift" and "Phoenix." Each of these contains a series of pieces that help the reader navigate the pain and joy of life's seasons.

For a personal and historical look at America during the Hippie Movement and beyond, you will find Shari's memoir, "Becoming Ruth," contributes a close look at the hearts and hurts, hopes and dreams, grit and grace of several generations of Americans.

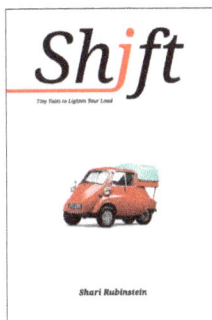

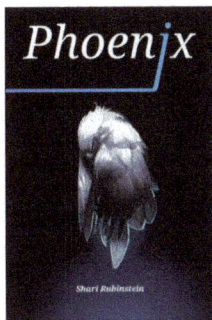

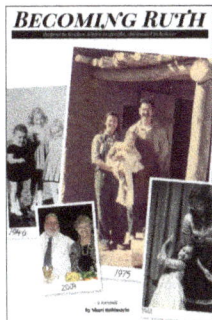

To learn more about these books
and read previews visit her website!

- *selah* -